Boomhood

BOOMHOOD

A Baby Boomer's Free-Range Childhood

Robert B. Hafey

Boomhood © Robert B. Hafey. All Rights Reserved, except where otherwise noted.

Copyright © 2017 Robert B. Hafey. All rights reserved. Printed in the United States of America.

Published by Robert B. Hafey
rbhafey@gmail.com

No part of this publication may be reproduced, distributed, stored in a database or retrieval system, or transmitted in any form or by any means, including photocopying, recording, or other electronic or mechanical methods, without the prior written permission of the publisher, except in the case of brief quotations embodied in critical reviews and certain other noncommercial uses permitted by copyright law. For permission requests, write to the publisher, addressed "Attention: Permission Requests," at the address below.

13915 Lemont Road
Homer Glen, Illinois 60491

Limit of Liability/Disclaimer of Warranty: The contents of this book are based solely on my flawed memory, which means others may recall some of the stories differently.

Visit the author's website at www.boomhood.com
www.facebook.com/boomhoodbook

First Edition
ISBN 978-0-9991032-0-3 (e-book)
ISBN 978-0-9991032-1-0 (paperback)

Cover by Kristen Gurnitz Bernier
Proofreading and copyediting by Ellen Sieminski

For all children. May you have a childhood that includes the freedom to explore and discover so you become independent, free-thinking, and creative adults.

Contents

Preface
xi

Acknowledgements
xiii

Introduction
1

Family and Place
5

Exploring the Natural World
19

Wait, What are Donuts Made of?
35

Size Matters
55

The Green Banana
71

Cursing the Astronauts
85

It Takes Faith to be an Angel
101

A Handful of Worm Poop
117

Chorizo Opened the Door to the World
135

And Here's the Beatles
155

Freedom to be me
169

Chapter References
171

About the Author
173

Preface

This memoir covers only my childhood. It begins with my earliest memories and then meanders along before concluding with my four years of military service. The written material is not organized in a sequential fashion in which I walk the reader through each succeeding year of my early life. Instead, the occurrences and experiences of my childhood have been organized under some subtle themes that unify the material into chapters that allow the reader to connect with the stories being told.

    I have authored two other books, both technical in nature, which had a limited audience due do the subject matter. The experience of writing those books gave me the courage to write this memoir. Writing a memoir was a fun learning experience, which allowed me to reflect on my childhood and begin to understand how it influenced and shaped me. During the two-plus years of writing, reflecting, and re-writing that it took to complete the manuscript, it became clear how my beliefs and actions have been influenced by the experiences of my free-range childhood.

    This is not a book of immense grief, sadness, or drama. It is simply a book about a child's often-fun experiences that everyone can and will identify with. Writing it helped me understand me. My intent is to help others understand themselves. If you are a baby boomer, reading this book may cause some soul-searching as you reflect on your free-range childhood and consider how it has made you the person you are today. For boomers and non-boomers alike, this book demonstrates that you can better understand others when learning about their experiences.

I believe everyone has a story to tell. I hope this book inspires others to tell theirs.

Acknowledgements

Writing this memoir would have been impossible without the shared memories created during my childhood. My parents, three brothers, five sisters, cousins, schoolmates, neighbors, fellow scouts, gang of friends, and fellow airmen all unknowingly contributed to the material in this book.

Not long after the beginning of the writing project a friend, Hank Hines, offered to read through a part of the jumbled mess I had concocted and then told me it was "good." He may not have been telling the complete truth, but he made me feel great.

Family members and friends also read sections of the manuscript as I was writing and re-writing. Their encouragement and kind words motivated me to continue the struggle. Two writing professionals from the Creative Nonfiction organization provided invaluable feedback that motivated me and keep the project moving forward.

Mike Cunningham, an English professor and good friend, read through as much of the manuscript as he could bear, offering feedback that redirected my efforts and was instrumental in the decision to organize the material into a chapter format.

My niece Kristen Gurnitz Bernier, a professional graphic artist, designed a book cover we are proud of. I truly enjoyed the back and forth dialogue that allowed the final cover design to emerge from our discussions.

Ellen Sieminski, a friend with boundless energy and intelligence, provided proofreading and copyediting assistance. The final product reflects her ability to focus on the details.

I am forever grateful to my wife Sandra, who was patient and understanding as I spent two-plus years either in front of my laptop or babbling endlessly about my childhood stories.

Introduction

Starting nine months after the end of World War II, the soldiers who had returned home to tightly embrace their wives and girlfriends began to frequent hospital maternity waiting rooms across the country. Their pent-up sexual desire, along with an optimistic view of the future saw the U.S. population balloon by 76 million from 1946 to 1964. Born in 1946, I and everyone sharing my birth year were on the leading edge of the boom – the first to qualify to use the generational descriptive term "baby boomer." By the time the baby boom ended in 1964, I was eighteen years old and prepared to move out into the world and make a difference.

The early years of my childhood, an age of innocence, occurred during a time of optimistic prosperity in the United States. A great war, which was preceded by a great depression, had just ended and the country was steeped in optimism.

By the time I turned 18 in 1964, that optimism began to wane. It began with the assassination of President John F. Kennedy in 1963. Then, in just a few years, the United States would be hopelessly mired in the unpopular Vietnam War and two more great men would be assassinated. Yet my childhood wasn't defined by a term describing a generation of post-World-War-II births or those landmark occurrences from the 1960s. It is instead a collection of experiences linked to the places I lived and the people with whom I interacted during my early years. Some experiences were unique to me, such as contracting rheumatic fever at the age 14, while others were common to everyone from this generation. For instance, recalling when the first television arrived in our home and remembering the first show we watched (*The Lone Ranger*; Hi-ho, Silver!) Or knowing exactly where we were when John F. Kennedy was shot (high school cafeteria) or when Neal Armstrong stepped onto the surface of the moon (U.S. Air Force barracks in the Philippines). This post-war and post-depression time period framed my childhood. That structural framework, when combined with my childhood experiences, formed the foundation for the person I am today.

During the years and decades that have passed since my childhood, the term "baby boomer" has taken on more of a cultural context. My generation is, in part, defined by some specific values or attributes that can be directly linked back to our childhood. There are three I hope to explore as the story of my childhood unfolds – optimism, independence, and exploration. I believe the sense of optimism we possessed was instilled in us by our parents. They had all just endured the hardships of the Great Depression and World War II. It was their optimism for the future that drove the increased birth rates that created our baby boomer generation. Comprising 40% of the population, we influenced or redirected our country into new and defining directions. The anti-war protests that helped to end the Vietnam War impacted not just this country, but the broader world as well. We were independent in our thinking and in our actions. We wanted to define a new way forward that was different from the path taken by our conservative parents. After all, we were raised to believe anything was possible, and we bought into the concept. The independence we were granted as children supported our desire for exploration and achievement. Some achievements were broad and far-reaching, including the societal changes relative to women's and minority rights, while others were individual and small in scale, such as walking 50 miles in one day because President John F. Kennedy challenged us to do so.

My childhood, along with those of many baby-boomers, was a free-range childhood. Our back doors were like swinging gates that we left and entered as we wished. From an early age, we independently roamed far and wide without parental supervision or oversight. After being gone all day, if we didn't show up for dinner, our parents might raise their eyebrows and call our names from the back porch. Our parents trusted not just us, but the community and society in general to watch over and protect us. By giving us this gift of freedom, they allowed us to grow and develop into young adults who felt independent and optimistic because we had learned many of life's lessons via self-exploration and trial and error. Why did our parents sanction this? Was it just a result of the times in which they raised us? A time just after the great evils of World War II had been defeated and the home front seemed safer than ever. Or was it related to the fact that they were not exposed to the constant barrage of bad news from all over the globe via the internet, as parents are today? The effect of this damaging and relentless internet bombardment is comparable to the continuous bombing of London during World War II that kept parents from letting their children roam the streets. The bombs were, and the bad news today is, incessant and draining.

This mental "bad news" assault causes parents to worry about and be fearful of the possible bad situations that might occur, be over protective, and deny their children the freedom to explore and learn without parental interference. In addition, many parents also narrow their circle of friends to like-minded people. By doing so, their children's ability to learn about the broader, diverse world is further contracted. Because of the freedom and independence I was given, I developed confidence in myself and my abilities and have lived my life without fear and worry. The freedom to explore and learn helped shape me so I fit neatly into a diverse society, not just a fragmented piece of it. The timing of my childhood could not have been better, for it broadened my horizons and helped prepare me to understand and accept the larger, complex world in which we all live today. And today, more than ever, we need the children of the world to be independent, optimistic, and confidently ready to explore the opportunities that will make our world a better place.

Family and Place

The old saying that you can pick your friends but not your family was true in my case. I was part of a unique and large family composed of my parents and eight siblings. A new sibling appeared about every two years until I was 14 years old so it was easy to get lost in the crowd. My early childhood, the period from the time of my birth until the age of ten, was also interrupted by multiple location changes. Moving around can push a child in one of two directions. The inevitable uncertainty associated with picking up and moving can either drive personal growth or cause someone to become introverted or rebellious because of the many adjustments required to fit into each new place and the social circles it contains. Because of my young age these moves were beneficial, not detrimental; they provided opportunities to learn and grow.

One's immediate family and relatives should be very influential in their childhood development and yet, not in mine. Being the second oldest child meant loose reigns and little parental guidance. My mother was busy, maybe at times overwhelmed, raising a large family. My father was generally disengaged from the parenting process, sitting at a corner tavern most every night. Grandparents, who for many are role models and provide unconditional love, were not part of my childhood either. Both sets of grandparents were, and remained, strangers due to distance and their death. Despite all of that, my childhood, like yours, was as unique as the geometric pattern within a single snowflake blowing past in a blizzard. From a distance, both wind-driven snowflakes and all our childhoods might look similar, so one needs to get very close and look hard to distinguish one from another.

...

My life's journey began on October 1, 1946. My parents did not wait for 1946, the first year of the baby boom, to begin their family. My entrance was upstaged by the 1944 birth of a sister in St. Augustine, FL. My father was serving in the military and stationed there at that time. I was born two years later in Harvey, Illinois, a suburb south of downtown Chicago. Living in Harvey, a town founded by a Christian leader that was intended to be a model town for Christians, created no lasting memories since we picked up and moved north shortly after my first birthday. My father, who was born in eastern North Dakota in the very small town of Monango, must have decided to take his family to the geographic area in which he felt most comfortable. Growing up in a small town with a peak population of 238 in 1920, the year before he was born, must have made cities like Chicago seem either oppressive and uninviting or exciting and energizing. Making the move implied he wanted to escape from big city life.

We settled not in Monango but in Fargo, ND, the state's largest city, where a second sister, the next of my eventual eight siblings, was born. I visited my father's birthplace and childhood home once. At the age of six we drove from our home in Minnesota back to Monango for his parents' 50th wedding anniversary celebration. Meeting my father's immediate family and his relatives at a very young age meant I retained no meaningful memories of them. Some visual memories that have remained are a farmyard containing a barn, a silo, and many free-range chickens and guinea fowl. A lesson about the intended use and ultimate value of these barnyard birds occurred not long after we arrived. While I watched with a mix of interest and angst, my grandfather corralled a nice plump hen and then proceeded to chop its head off with an axe while it was firmly held, against its will, on a tree stump. Although this common farm experience taught me that the saying, "running around like a chicken with its head cut off," is based on fact, the event caused my heart to race and made me feel so uncomfortable I quickly moved to my father's side for solace and reassurance. From that vantage point it was easy to observe both the bright, sunny summer day with brilliant blue skies and a now-headless chicken racing quietly across the barnyard until it fell to the ground, twitched for a few moments, and died. This was my first experience with death, if you discount the countless ants that I had mercilessly crushed or fried with a magnifying glass in our back yard.

The chicken butchering experience did nothing to strengthen the bonds between me and my axe-wielding grandfather. Fleeing the crime scene, my escape route took me back into the farmhouse where the cinnamon and sugar smell coming from an apple pie baking in my grandmother's wood-fired kitchen stove stopped me in my tracks. Walking near the stove and absorbing the scorching heat radiating from its black cast iron surfaces was like standing in the hot August sun. It was uncomfortably warm yet the smell of the pie kept me frozen there until my cheeks reddened. The pie, served after the fresh chicken dinner, was so good it made me forget the murder witnessed earlier in the day. As the sky darkened and the grieving barnyard chickens retreated to their coop, I ascended some creaking stairs, reaching high to grasp the wood-spindle-supported handrail. I entered my bedroom, old enough to know I was sleeping someplace different, but young enough to not care. Laying there in the still darkness I was ready for sleep to erase the memories of the day.

The next day we attended my grandparents' anniversary party, which was held at a school hall right across the street from their house. Music, food and strangers filled the afternoon. When the party ended, our family departed for home, leaving behind relatives I would never see again. My father's parents and his extended family remained strangers, for during the balance of my childhood there was zero contact with them. As a child, these broken branches on my family tree had no meaning, but today there is a yearning for information. My father did not talk about his past during my childhood. Later in life, when asked about his early years, he would retreat to his lifelong refuge, a glass of beer, and quickly withdraw from the possible conversation.

From Fargo, it was a short move to Mankato, in south central Minnesota, where we lived for a few years before relocating to the even smaller town of St. Peter, Minnesota. My parents may have believed they were solely responsible for creating the "baby boom," or they were simply overly optimistic about what the future held, and the family expansion continued in Minnesota where a brother and two more sisters were born. My father changed jobs frequently and we changed residences almost as often, living in at least four different rental homes. The first place, the home where my earliest childhood memories were formed, was a small, white, wood-frame home that was on the outskirts of Mankato where homes were sparse and open spaces were abundant. On calm, warm summer nights I would lie in bed and peer into the darkness through my bedroom window screen. While watching for the sporadic glow of lightning bugs, the sounds of the neighborhood drifted into my room and kept me from falling asleep. Our small house was just three houses in from a two-lane highway so the steady hum of traffic was always in the background. So was the sound of music; on the other side of the highway was a drive-in restaurant. It had inside seating along with covered parking spots. Customers would pull in and then be waited on by car hops who would deliver their orders on trays that would balance on partially raised car windows. Outside speakers filled the night with whatever popular tune of the day was playing on the jukebox inside. A Sheb Wooley song titled "The Purple People Eater" did nothing to stimulate sleep and for the next few days I kept watch for individuals with only one eye. My only memory of eating out in a restaurant with my family was sitting with my parents inside this drive-in restaurant when very young. Before eating the hamburger my father had ordered for me, the sound of the beef patties sizzling and caramelizing on a flat-top griddle filled the air. Wafting from that hot surface and filling the restaurant was a smell that still defines what great hamburgers smell like.

As our family and financial problems grew we moved into a new rental home in Mankato and eventually to the nearby small town of St. Peter, MN where we lived in a Quonset hut. A Quonset hut is a prefabricated structure made from corrugated galvanized steel with a semi-circle cross section. If a very large tin can was cut in half vertically and then the two halves were laid on the ground you would have two miniature Quonset huts. These huts that ran along a street in St. Peter were probably subsidized housing. As a young child, any awareness of our financial situation or the reason why we moved from place to place did not exist. For me each move meant new territory with different places to explore. Right next to the row of Quonset huts was a large park containing a baseball diamond that was the home field of the St. Peter Saints. They were a semi-pro baseball team that provided free entertainment on both hot summer afternoons and warm, humid nights. When attending the games, my time was spent under the stands looking up rather than watching the action. As the baseball fans dropped their soda and beer bottles, neighborhood kids, including me, would scramble to retrieve the empties in order to collect the bottle deposit from the concession stand. Looking up gave you a head start on the others when a bottle dropped and it also prevented you from getting conked on the head. At five cents per bottle it was like panning for gold – you never knew how much money you could rake in. Learning early that life isn't always about having fun or being entertained was a lesson carried away with the nickels in my pocket.

One of the most unforgettable memories, and now family lore, from living at this location has to do with a chicken named Henry. During my early childhood, for a few weeks before Easter, an individual could purchase cute, cuddly baby rabbits and chicks from retail outlets. Their fur and feathers had been dyed the colors of the season – intense pink, purple, bright yellow and powder blue, which caused me and every other child to pester our parents for one. It is unclear how my older sister obtained the chick she named Henry, but like all children who receive a pet, she quickly became emotionally attached to the adorable, colorful hatchling. As Henry grew and fledged out it became obvious to everyone that he had been given an appropriate male name and would not be producing any eggs for our breakfast meals. Henry was a young rooster and once he began to crow, he started at first light. Our family may have tolerated this commotion, but since we were living in a row of Quonset huts that were built within very close proximity of each other, the neighbors would not. The wake up calls at the crack of dawn annoyed them and they began to complain to our parents. It was obvious to my parents that Henry had to be disposed of and money was tight. One of my mother's regular recipes was for pan-fried chicken. She often served her version of this moist, succulent chicken dish for our Sunday meal and the next Sunday was no exception. After being killed, plucked, butchered, salted, peppered, and dredged in flour, Henry was slowly and skillfully sautéed for about 50 minutes. When done, he rested on a plate while the pan drippings were turned into milk gravy to accompany the mashed potatoes. Henry fed the entire family, except for my tearful older sister, who refused to eat. My North Dakota grandfather had taught me what chickens were for. I enjoyed the dinner and asked for seconds since my sister wasn't partaking.

Our last Minnesota residence was a vacation cabin that was part of a fishing resort located on a nearby lake. Since it was fall, and the resort season was over, the owners agreed to rent one of the cabins to my parents, who were still struggling financially. As a child, it seemed to me like a neat place to live. Most kids might get to go to a fishing resort for a summer vacation, yet here we were living at one! It was about this time that I started to become aware of the fact that our family was struggling to make ends meet. Frequent parental arguments about money and my father's inability to hold a steady job began to have meaning. Indicators like eating boiled rice with milk, cinnamon and sugar for breakfast, because that is all we had, reinforced our financial situation. We rode a school bus to and from school and after school we were dropped off by the resort driveway. Some older children on the bus made fun of us because we lived at a fishing resort. At my age I couldn't explain exactly why we did but I remember getting off the bus in a hurry, feeling embarrassed and running up the long driveway. Before getting to our cabin home I passed some mature apple trees on the resort property. It was early fall and the trees were slumping under the weight of hundreds of beautiful apples with skins colored a mix of green and red. Picking one and polishing it against my shirt caused the deep red section to shine like a mirror. While holding the apple close to my face, a faint reflection of a sad boy was visible. Biting into its juicy, crisp flesh and tasting the subtle sweetness helped to ease my sadness.

Our lack of financial resources might have driven one of my sisters and me to commit larceny on less than a grand scale while living at the resort. Like most resorts, there was a small concession area where the guests could purchase soft drinks and snacks, including potato chips and candy. On one occasion, the two of us stealthily climbed through an open window when no one was around, to access the concession area and steal a box of Black Crows – a thimble-shaped, soft, black licorice candy. With our stolen candy in hand we reversed our trail and escaped to the outside of the building where we soberly yet happily ate the entire box. If caught, the black bits lodged between our teeth along with our licorice breath would have been evidence enough to convict us. To this day a piece of black licorice, or a glass of really good red wine that has some licorice overtones, can trigger a slight sense of guilt only a young criminal would understand.

Just after finishing fourth grade, we once again picked up and moved. This time we relocated to another state – the state of Illinois where I had been born nine years earlier. My father had difficulty holding a steady job and my grandfather had suffered a stroke a few years earlier and needed someone to look after him. My parents, or maybe just my mother, decided to move back to Joliet and her family. When the school year ended our possessions and still-growing family were packed up. We journeyed south to take up residence in my grandfather's home, where my mother was raised, located at 500 Francis Street in Joliet, Illinois.

Where we live in this country helps to define who we are and how we will fit into and accept the broader world. The cultural norms, beliefs, and prejudices we are exposed to while growing up can be blinders that narrow our view of the world. On the unhappy drive to Illinois, the awareness that my range was expanding and my opportunity to explore and learn would be greatly extended did not enter my mind. Travel at this point in my life meant being uprooted and relocating to a strange new place. As an adult the opportunity to travel and see many other parts of the world has opened my eyes to the world. I now fully understand the value of travel relative to my view of the people who populate our world. Travel is not checking off a list of the local tourist sites. That is tourism. Travel is about experiencing the culture of a place. Culture to me is how people think, act, and interact. Relocating to Joliet meant having to adapt my behaviors and actions to fit in and to be open to learning from the new experiences I would be exposed to.

Departing Minnesota, we drove off into the dark unknown. My emotions ranged from anxiety and worry to sadness and grief when I thought about leaving the places and friends, including my dog Sparky, which had defined home for me. At my age there was no choice other than to accept my parents' decision. The long drive south created only one distinct memory. As we drove along Interstate 90 in central Wisconsin there were some limestone bluffs and a natural limestone tower that were unique. Passing them today causes me to pause and remember myself as a young boy staring out of the back window of my parents' car. Although briefly distracted by the scenic beauty, I was very concerned about the uncertainty that awaited me in Joliet.

The Joliet home into which we moved was owned by my grandfather. By the time we arrived, his wife, my grandmother, had been dead for a few years and my grandfather, having suffered a severe stroke, was confined to a wheelchair. My Joliet grandparents had emigrated from a region in Eastern Europe that is now part of Slovakia and formerly Austria. My grandfather's first job after emigrating to the U.S. was laboring in a coal mine in central Illinois. From there he moved to Joliet where he was employed by the EJ&E (Elgin, Joliet and Eastern) Railroad as a carpenter. His house was a wooden frame structure that had six rooms and only one bath. The front and back doors were aligned in an almost straight line. If you entered through the front door, the bedrooms and bathroom were to the left and a living room, dining room, and kitchen on the right. All of the bedrooms were small, with the beds taking up a majority of the floor space.

The living room was the communal space where we would gather to watch TV. My favorite viewing position was lying on the floor with my arms under my head. While lying there one Sunday night, the Beatles made their first appearance on the Ed Sullivan variety show and it caused me to sit straight up and realize this was something special. One show that scared the crap out of me was Alfred Hitchcock Presents. All of the shows in the series were kind of murder mysteries that kept you on the edge of your seat – or in my case twitching on the floor in front of the television. The TV was a shared resource for a large family so my siblings and I rarely had a choice in what we watched. In the evenings my mother made the choices, but after school the Three Stooges entertained me until my older sister arrived home, strong armed me, and then switched channels to view American Bandstand hosted by Dick Clark. Our dining room was rarely used for dining, with the exception of a few holidays, but the table was used to do homework, play board games and put together jig-saw puzzles. We ate our meals in the kitchen at a table barely large enough to hold our sizable family. The bathroom contained a cast iron bathtub that was a refuge in a house filled with so many people. Soaking in the hot water until it was cold provided solitude and solace. There were also stairs leading to an attic and a scary basement. Scary because it containing a fire-breathing demon of a coal-burning furnace. Every month or so during the winter, a truck would pull up to our house and discharge a black dusty load of coal down a chute that led to a coal bin located in the basement. The furnace was troublesome and my father failed to inherit a "handy gene," so he struggled to keep it running. This meant many cold mornings and more than one day without heat in the house. Eventually a natural gas conversion unit was installed to tame the demon furnace and hot air from the discharge vents became a regular occurrence. The attic, a space with visible ceiling and roof joists, remained unused until after my departure when a younger brother turned part of it into a bedroom to escape the chaos below.

    The back door of the house led to a rectangular back porch that was almost as long as the house was wide. My most lasting memory related to the porch is of my grandfather sitting there in his wheelchair on warm summer days. He was partially paralyzed from the stroke he had suffered and therefore could not walk unaided or communicate effectively. I did not know him before the stroke and didn't really know what having a stroke meant. The physical damage that resulted from his stroke made me a bit afraid of him. When he would get frustrated and angry he would shout incoherently. If he disapproved of my actions he would use his one good arm to shake his cane at me, which caused me to stay clear of him. Occasionally, with his one good hand, he would pull out a small coin pouch and extract a dime before calling me over and with great difficulty mouth the word "Twinkies." He would deposit the dime into my outstretched hand and then shake his cane at me to get me going. After running to a small neighborhood grocery store to purchase a two-pack of Twinkies, I'd return and hand him his sweet treat. Pinning the package under his paralyzed arm, he would use his good hand to wrestle open the cellophane packaging and then extract and slowly eat both Twinkies with a twinkle in his eye. I understood he did not have an easy life and having a sweet treat meant a lot to him. He is genetically partly responsible for my addiction to sweets and I wish we could have shared a Twinkie or two together, but he never offered.

On other occasions he would pull out the same coin pouch, extract some change, and send me to the store for a pouch of Redman chewing tobacco. If he wasn't eating a meal, savoring a Twinkie, or sleeping, he was chewing and spitting. Next to his wheelchair was an old coffee can into which he would discharge the brown spittle. Chewing tobacco must have provided some pleasure, but his weakly projected spittle, and the resulting chin dribble, was another reason for me to keep my distance. When I moved into the house he was already an old, broken man who was unable to share his knowledge, his passions or anything else with me. He did teach me that having a stroke will destroy your life as you knew it. This caused me to fear the same fate, as he is part of my genetic pool. Not long after we moved in my grandfather died in bed. An ambulance was called and a priest visited to administer the last rights before his body was removed from the house. I didn't feel sad because I had not experienced human death before and no strong bond existed between us. Bonds have to be broken for tears to flow – therefore, none were shed.

When my family moved into my grandfather's house, the household census took a dramatic turn upward from one to nine. There were only three bedrooms; my grandfather briefly occupied one of them and my parents another. So unlike many of today's children who believe it is their birth right to have their own bedroom, my experience was sharing a small bedroom with some of my eventual eight siblings. Living in these tight conditions was one of the motivations that pushed me to explore the world around me and become independent.

This house on the East side of Joliet is where I experienced the happenings of everyday life that, when distilled, created my largest collection of childhood memories. Many of these childhood recollections are vague and clouded by the years of adult experiences layered on top of them. Others are as clear as the day they occurred. Those Joliet memories make up the bulk of my story and it is important to understand Joliet's early history for it has relevance to my individual story. The Encyclopedia of Chicago describes the history of the town as follows:

In 1673 Louis Jolliet and Father Jacques Marquette paddled up the Des Plaines River and camped on a huge mound a few miles south of present-day Joliet.

In 1833 following the Black Hawk War, Charles Reed built a cabin along the west side of the Des Plaines River. Across the river in 1834 James B. Campbell, treasurer of the canal commissioners, laid out the village of "Juliet," a name local settlers had been using before his arrival.

The Juliet region was part of Cook County until 1836, when it became the county seat of the new Will County. Just before the depression of 1837, Juliet incorporated as a village, but to cut tax expenses, Juliet residents soon petitioned the state to rescind that incorporation.

In 1845 local residents changed the community's name from "Juliet" to "Joliet." Joliet was reincorporated as a city in 1852. Soon, Joliet's transportation arteries included the Des Plaines River, a road that followed the Sauk Trail, the Illinois & Michigan Canal (1848), and the Rock Island Railroad (1852), which ran through the business district. Today Joliet is served by several railroads, as well as Interstate Highways 55 and 80, which intersect a few miles southwest of the city.

The quarrying of limestone, with a bluish-white tinge, earned

Joliet the nickname "City of Stone." The Illinois & Michigan Canal was both a consumer of stone in the building of locks, bridges, and aqueducts and, after its completion in 1848, an artery for shipping stone to regional customers.

In 1858 the state of Illinois located a new penitentiary in Joliet, in part because of the abundance of stone for prison walls and cell houses. The Chicago Fire of 1871 spurred demand for stone and by 1890, Joliet quarries were shipping over three thousand railroad carloads of stone per month to Chicago and other cities.

The "City of Steel" emerged with the construction of the Joliet mill in 1869. The Bessemer converters installed at the mill in the 1870s were among the earliest used in the United States. While canal construction drew Irish immigrants, the steel mill attracted thousands of southeastern Europeans. These new immigrants also found jobs on the railroad that serviced the steel mill, the Elgin, Joliet & Eastern Railway. (Encyclopedia of Chicago)

How is Joliet's history connected to my story? My grandfather was one of those Eastern European immigrants who worked at the EJ&E Railroad. My first full-time job was at the local steel mill. I hiked and hunted along the towpaths of the Illinois & Michigan Canal and many limestone structures and one of the limestone quarries were within a quarter mile of my home. Joliet's history and my history are intertwined. My Joliet home and the neighborhood in which it was located were like the sets in a play where the experiences of my childhood took place. These sets give life to the stories that describe my journey from childhood to an optimistic and independent adult.

Exploring the Natural World

Throughout my childhood I independently, or with friends, continually explored my natural surroundings. The place where my free-range childhood began, and the home where my earliest childhood memories were formed, was a small, white, wood-frame house located on the outskirts of Mankato, MN. A prominent feature of this rental home was a large garden that filled the backyard. My parents planted a variety of vegetables in the garden and as they were nurtured, grew and developed, I did the same. As my confidence grew, my desire to explore increased and my range expanded from the backyard of our home to the surrounding neighborhood and beyond. Lessons to be learned were everywhere around me.

A short walk down a two-lane blacktop road from our home was an uninhabited section of the Minnesota River. Here, where it made a sweeping, broad bend, it had shallow, sandy shorelines with weedy sections that were ideal for a young boy to explore. While walking down the sloped bank, I visually scanned the river for signs of life. Occasionally, Mallard or Black ducks, who were surprised by my appearance, would take to the air following an almost vertical leap from the water's surface. I recall taking off my shoes and socks and walking slowly through the weedy shallows. I would catch long-nose turtles, which had smooth, soft, rubbery shells and funny-looking long, pointed noses, as well as tri-colored leopard frogs. After capturing either one it was cradled in my small hands for a closer examination before it was released back into the slow current of the river. The frogs would frantically swim away to take up a positon underwater while the turtles would slowly swim from my hands and then, as they drifted away in the river's gurgling current, poke their head above the water to peer back at their former captor. Smelling my hands hours later, the dried, musky residue these amphibians left behind transported me back to the river's edge.

Between our home and the river was an open field with an old, abandoned orchard, which was another place to explore. What remained of the old orchard were mostly broken fragments of barren apple trees and a few almost-lifeless plum trees that struggled to bear fruit. On hot summer days, my older sister and I picked up and ate the most delicious plums that had fallen to the ground. Each bite of those sun-warmed, overripe, sweet, red-skinned plums caused sticky yellow juice to run down our faces and onto our hands. We looked at each other with joy on our smudged faces, believing we were eating candy.

Every fall, while in the woods or walking along roadways, nuts that had fallen to the ground attracted me. Round, green balls would litter the ground under Black Walnut trees. They had a unique smell unlike anything else, which caused me to pick them up, scratch their surface, and sniff the scent. Then as the cool fall days passed, the exterior of the rock-hard globes would slowly turn from green to a blotchy brownish-yellow and finally to a mushy black. When very young, I once tried extracting the nuts from their rotting exterior with my hands. For the next few days my hands appeared to have been tattooed by a drunken tattoo artist, for they had a mottled, multi-racial look. That experience taught me to step on the mushy black exterior in order to push out the rock-hard walnut that was hidden within. Following the extraction step, the nuts were collected in a paper grocery bag and left to dry for a few weeks. The next and hardest step in this foraging adventure was to extract the nut meat from the rock-hard shell. Sitting on a sidewalk, with my legs spread-eagle, each nut was pummeled with multiple hammer blows until it cracked or exploded into fragments. Just before the hammer head contacted the walnut, I would close my eyes or look away to avoid any shrapnel. Inside of each shell was a maze-like structure that contained the object of my effort – the nutmeat. It was impossible to extract large pieces because the hammer blows not only pulverized the shell, but also the nut meat. Resisting the urge to eat my collection of nut fragments, the pieces were gathered and deposited into a cup. A few hours of work would yield about one cup of nut pieces, which were delivered to my mother. Within a day or two of my delivery she would perfume our house with the buttery, caramelized-sugar scent of baking banana bread containing the black walnuts. The walnuts added an indescribable unique flavor.

My explorations often found me just lying in a field or sitting in the woods and doing nothing but observing my surroundings. During the hot summer, the orchard and surrounding open fields had specific sights, smells, and sounds that, when sensed today, transport me quickly back in time. Particular wild flowers and weeds, under the hot July or August sun, gave off scents that were unique. Laying on my belly in large patches of clover, while scanning the patch for the illusive four-leaf clover, permanently engrained the sweet, fragrant smell of clover flowers into my olfactory memory and gave me a clear understanding of what "busy as a bee" meant. Just inches from my face, hectic honey bees would fly from flower to flower to harvest both the clover flowers' nectar and the yellow pollen that clung in large, bulging clumps to their rear legs. For years to come, before spreading Sue Bee clover honey on a piece of toast, the jar was lifted to my nose so the faint scent of clover flowers could be remembered. Another plant that was prevalent in these fields was a rather spindly, sparsely-foliaged plant. It grew to the size of a small, scraggly bush and starting in July it was covered in spiked white or yellow floral shoots. The mild scent of their flowers is something unforgettable. In the heat of every summer since my early childhood, when the scent from this prairie plant is detected, it instantly transports me back to those fields in Minnesota. Milkweed plants were a summer-long wonder. Breaking open one of their leaves or stems caused the plant to bleed a sticky white substance that remained on my hands until they were washed. Tearing open their large, comma-shaped seed pods in the fall allowed me to watch in amazement as the seeds, anchored to the bottom of a silky, umbrella-like structure, drifted off on the lightest of breezes. Milkweeds attract Monarch butterflies, for it is the plant onto which they deposit their eggs. When in bloom, the perfume they released from their circular bulb of tiny, bluish-purple flowers was the most aromatic and intoxicating scent in the summer prairie. It is unclear to me if butterflies can smell, but if they can, this is how they locate these plants to lay their eggs.

Along with a variety of colorful yellow and orange butterflies, grass hoppers were an abundant insect in the prairie fields. The butterflies would always land and let me look, but as soon as they sensed my hand reaching toward them they fluttered off to land on another flowering plant. The grasshoppers started out small and were easy to catch and examine in mid-summer. But by the late summer they had developed into winged giants that easily avoided my young hands as they flew away making a kind of a whirring, clicking sound. When a small one was caught, and I could resist to the urge to quickly release it as it tickled the palm of my hand, it would leave a small stain of brown liquid that my friends and I called tobacco juice. In reality, the capture may have scared the shit out of them! Another common prairie plant had very small white flowers that were part of a lacy, flat flower head. Pulling on the stem of this plant made my hands smell like carrots. That prompted me to pull one of the plants out of the ground to examine the root. It was small and whitish. When bent, a strong carrot aroma was released. The fear of poisoning myself kept me from putting it into my mouth for a taste.

The birds that occupied my areas of exploration did not get my attention until one early fall day while exploring a heavily wooded area. A group of large blue-, black-, and white-colored birds with crests on their heads were repeatedly calling loudly. This caused me to sit down and watch them. They moved into the woods and took turns flying toward a large tree and diving at something while they screamed loudly and repeatedly. The commotion went on for minutes while the reason for their anger remained a mystery. Finally, a very large bird that had been the object of their attention flushed from the tree and flew off toward a new section of the woods. As it silently glided away the shrieking attackers followed in close pursuit. Sitting there puzzled by what I had just witnessed, the mob of birds could again be heard renewing their attack. This unique solitary experience made me feel giddy with wonder and excitement.

My early explorations of the fields and woods in Minnesota were often under a sky full of small, white, puffy clouds that seemed to be, just like my childhood, effortlessly floating by. Clouds, like natural features in the terrain, can be common to a location and stir memories of that location. From this point in time all of my early-childhood, natural-sensory memories seem frozen in time. I can easily reconnect with my past through the smells, sights, and sounds of the natural memories that were formed as I spent uninterrupted time alone taking in my natural surroundings.

My outdoor experiences also included hunting and fishing. Hunting and fishing played an important role in my development, for they taught me about responsibility. In addition, my optimistic spirit was fed by the anticipation felt while hunting and fishing, as both of those activities were lessons in hope. Unless one is exposed to hunting and fishing as a child, it is unlikely he or she will participate in these activities as an adult. Since my father grew up in rural North Dakota where he hunted and fished, he introduced me to both as a young child. My introduction to hunting occurred when my father returned home from a waterfowl hunt with two musty-smelling dead ducks. One of them was a male Mallard with a head full of the most beautiful iridescent green feathers. The other was a Pintail duck that had a body covered in feathers with geometric patterns that caused me to stare in wonder. They intrigued me because of their beauty – even in death. As he plucked and cleaned the two ducks, his actions reminded me of his own father cleaning the chicken he had butchered just a year or so earlier. In both cases it was dirty, smelly work.

My earliest fishing memory is of me and my father sitting in a boat on a lake in Minnesota under clear blue skies. We were fishing for crappies and together we caught a stringer full. Crappies are a white and black mottled pan fish with small mouths that can be tricky to hook. The good news is they tend to congregate together in schools so when you locate them you have a chance of catching a mess of fish. We did and when we returned home my father gave me a quick lesson in scaling and cleaning fish. Scaling the fish caused the slime-covered, iridescent scales to fly everywhere in random, unpredictable flight patterns like shooting stars in the night sky. Hours later they would be found stuck to my clothing, arms and hair. Cleaning the fish really meant cutting off the head and removing the guts. This was a rather gruesome task for a young boy. It didn't take long to understand why my father departed to have a cold beer while cleaning the fish was left for me. Catching is much more fun than cleaning.

Fishing for bullheads was another fond memory. To catch the bullheads we fished on the bottom of a very small river using worms or pieces of chicken liver for bait. Invariably, when a bullhead was caught it had swallowed the hook which meant having to handle the fish while trying to extract the hook from deep in its throat. That could be a painful experience for both of us, for if mishandled, the bullheads' saw-toothed spines would puncture my hand. That painful stinging sensation created a memory that still causes me to cringe. Cleaning a bullhead was also a unique experience because they had no scales. Instead of scaling a fish, pliers were used to firmly grip its skin and pull it off before removing its head and entrails. All of my fishing experiences as a child made it very clear where fish came from and what was required to prepare them for the dining table. Whenever there was a catch, my mother would lightly bread and then pan fry the fish. With a sense of pride, I would tuck into their succulent flesh before eating my favorite part – the crispy tail that tasted like a fishy potato chip.

The Minnesota lakes where we fished contained other creatures. When swimming in the cold lake water, it was always easy to warm up after walking onto the shore and discovering the leeches that had attached themselves to my legs. As one of my parents pulled the leeches off, blood would run down my leg from their attachment point. The fear felt while this was taking place caused an immediate warming of my cold extremities. Years later, while using leeches for walleye fishing bait, no sorrow was felt as I threaded them onto a hook. Another pest associated with my rambling explorations in the fields and woods of Minnesota was the tick. Dogs and kids like me were easy targets for these blood-sucking insects. Petting the dog would lead to the discovery of bloated ticks that had swelled with blood until they were the size of a pea. When my parents discovered a tick on me, the approved removal method was to heat their ass with the end of a lit cigarette. Mom or dad would simply light up, take a drag, knock off the ashes and then apply the cigarette to the tick's behind. With this subtle encouragement, it would extract itself from my flesh so it could be crushed. Despite the leeches and ticks, outdoor activities were a fun and important part of my early childhood development in Minnesota.

When my parents made the decision to move back to Illinois, my birth state, we drove off into the unknown and my landscape completely changed. The clean lakes, rivers, and open fields that were explored in Minnesota were left behind. My new neighborhood, in industrial Joliet, was block after block of homes and businesses. The clean, crisp, cold winter air of Minnesota was replaced with the smell of burning coal and a snowy landscape covered with coal soot. Seeing the Hamm's beer commercials on television with the jingle about the Land of Sky Blue Waters caused me to feel homesick. That jingle caused me to visualize my former free-range sites and the white, puffy clouds floating effortlessly above them. Nonetheless, since change is the only constant, I had to let go of the past and accept my new reality.

Soon after we were settled in our Joliet home and neighborhood, my interest in nature drove me to explore my new surroundings. My starting point was Heggie hills, an old industrial wasteland bordered by Heggie Park, a run-down manufacturing site and a coal yard. The hills and ponds that made up Heggie hills did not naturally occur due to the glacial retreat thousands of years ago. The hills were actually man-made excavation deposits piled up next to the small ponds that filled with water after the digging occurred. The digging must have happened decades earlier and may have been exploratory digs looking for limestone deposits that could be quarried. The hills had limestone outcroppings and were littered with chunks of limestone rock. There were many old homes, along with the nearby Collins Street Prison, which were constructed entirely of Joliet limestone blocks. More than one limestone quarries existed in Joliet. Within the boundaries of the nearby prison property was a massive quarry from which the limestone used to construct the prison's twenty-five-foot tall and five-foot-thick walls had been quarried. It was less than a quarter mile from where we played in Heggie hills. My friends and I never gave a thought to how the Heggie hills were created, but whomever was responsible for creating this secret world that existed outside the view of our parents deserved our everlasting gratitude. For me this open land was a nature center.

There were four ponds located in the hills, which were the

source of an unending biology education. Walking down to the ponds was like entering a secret hiding place since they were lower than the surround landscape. I moved cautiously to prevent loose stones from tumbling down the path and into the pond, for that would frighten the subjects of my nature study. On hot, steamy summer days a notable increase in temperature could be felt at pond level because the surrounding hills blocked any cooling breeze. From the pond's edge, where it was quiet and still, I stood motionless day after day while observing the complete growth cycle of frogs. It began with the smallest of tadpoles, swimming in little black clouds along the pond shore. They soon transformed into small frogs with their tadpole tails still attached and then finally into fully grown green, black and tan leopard frogs that would spring into the ponds when frightened by my movement. Most often they were not seen but only heard as their splayed bodies belly-flopped onto the moss-lined water's edge to escape underwater. Then within a few minutes, their heads poked through the green moss growing along the shoreline to scan the horizon for danger. The dragonflies and water spiders, which were abundant in these ponds, were a source of amazement. They both effortlessly, in a millisecond, darted in any direction they chose – one on the water and the other in the air. Clearly the dragonflies were flying, but the sight of water spiders skating across the water's surface always caused me to stop, watch, and try and understand the mystery. The ponds were science labs that taught me more about biology than my grade-school classes.

The rocky, limestone terrain of the hills meant snakes were an abundant species. One hot summer day I was running very fast on the downslope of an undulating path that crisscrossed the hills. While in midair and about to touch down on the path I saw a snake where my foot was going to land. If this situation had occurred prior to the Wright Brothers first flight I might have been acknowledged as the first person to fly. Fear caused me to will myself to levitate and fly forward another six inches to avoid the serpent. Snakes were, of course, a source of both fright and interest to us. We spent hours one early summer morning turning over slabs of limestone looking for and capturing young garden snakes. Fear taught me to use two sticks to corral and then lift them up. There must have been a bumper crop that spring, for we filled the bottom of a discarded metal pan with a slithering mass of serpents. Of course we were proud of our accomplishment and proceeded to Heggie Park to show off our catch to the neighborhood girls. A real interest in girls had not yet sparked in me and my friends, but little did we know we may have extinguished some relationships before they had a chance to ignite. None of us realized how loud girls could scream before that day and those blood-curdling screams may be, in part, responsible for our diminished hearing today.

On another day we discovered a wild beehive hanging from a low branch of a tree. We spent the next hour sharpening our pitching skills by hurling rocks from our vantage point on a nearby hillside toward the hive to drive this pestilence from our secret nature center. Rather than bee keepers, we were bee drivers. Eventually we, like hunter-gatherers of old, were rewarded for our efforts when we could approach the broken hive and taste the sweet honey directly from pieces of the honeycomb.

A new type of exploring occurred on an eighth-grade field trip to Springfield, Illinois to visit both Abraham Lincoln's tomb and the home in which he lived when elected president of the United States. Rather than on my own, or with a few friends, I found myself on a bus with my entire class. The long, grueling bus trip to and from Springfield consumed five hours of the day which meant our stops at the historic sites were short and rushed. The excitement felt when getting on the bus slowly faded as mile after mile of corn and soybean fields passed. The bus window reflection showed me staring blankly out of the window while listening to the steady hum of the bus tires against the concrete roadway. History had little meaning to me as a child, so I was not fully aware of the contributions Lincoln had made to our country. When we pulled up to the cemetery where his tomb was located, no emotions were stirred. Shortly after exiting the bus and walking around the tomb, we filed past a cast bronze bust of President Lincoln's head. As each person passed, he or she rubbed the nose of the casting, which had lost all of its patina and now glistened like a guiding light in the early summer sun. After rubbing his nose, which felt smooth and warm, I walked back to the bus while feeling a kind of awe not experienced before.

The next stop was Lincoln's Springfield home. We toured the empty residence and peered into the roped-off rooms to view the furnishings of that period. Being too young to appreciate "old," the antiques we observed in the rooms had no meaning to me. My mind began to envision the children who lived there, wondering what life was like for them. Our final stop, New Salem, had reconstructed log cabins akin to the one in which Lincoln lived as a young adult. Here, we sat at picnic tables and ate our lunch before piling back onto the bus for the trip home. On the long ride home, as my head pitched from side to side in unison with the motion of the bus, I thought about how this trip had been a different kind of exploration when compared to my childhood adventures. Exploring history and a person who made history was a good experience that left me longing for more.

My explorations of the outdoor areas near my home continued while in high school when a friend who owned a gun asked me to join him and his father on their hunting excursions. After my father agreed to a gun purchase, I became the proud owner of a well-used Mossberg bolt action 20-gauge shotgun. The stock was cracked and the safety was sketchy, but this gun provided me with many days of entertainment. Not long after, a few other friends were allowed to own or use their fathers' shotguns and we discovered our own hunting territory close to our neighborhood. On fall Saturday mornings, our group of young hunters would strike out and walk down the main commercial road, Collins Street, carrying our cloth-case-enclosed shotguns over our shoulders. Today, if we did this, a squad car would pull up with sirens blaring and light flashing while the officers, with guns drawn, would order us into spread-eagle positions against the side of the squad car. But in the early sixties we went on our merry way and no one thought anything of it. After the US Steel property and just before the Collins Street prison, we would hang a left on a short street that would take us to open lands behind the two properties. On one occasion, just before stepping across the railroad tracks that bordered the open land, I looked up and noticed a prison guard on duty in one of the lookout towers along the prison wall, watching us. We casually waved to each other just before my friends and I stepped into our hunting area next to the prison.

Our hunting area was bordered by commercial property on one side, a river and canal on the other, and ran for a few miles north to the city of Lockport. It contained the ruins of the old steel works and acre upon acre of grassy, scrubby terrain where we might kick up a rabbit or a ring-necked pheasant. Every step taken through clumps of grass or around small bushes provided endless hope, for any one step could cause a rabbit or pheasant to flush. It was rare to see game and even rarer to bring something home to clean and eat. The few times a cock pheasant flushed from cover in front of me, the view of its plumage, a startling mix of brilliant iridescent colors, stunned me as much as the noise it made. It literally took my breath away. Once when we were pushing our way through an area heavy with cattails, suddenly and without warning, a huge cock pheasant erupted from the cover in front of me. After raising my gun and releasing the safety, I looked down the barrel to align my shot. Immediately something other than the pheasant appeared in the line of fire. Off in the distance was the State Police building located along the highway. This wary old bird was flying directly in line with the building, causing me to pause and drop the gun barrel without firing. Had that wily old bird planned his escape route?

Since rabbit season paralleled pheasant season, we pursued both during our excursions. An area behind the US Steel plant was excellent rabbit-hunting terrain. The sparsely wooded area was open enough that you could see the rabbits run their zig-zag escape pattern before ducking into one of the many man-made cubby holes located there. These hiding places were the old concrete foundations for blast furnaces and other structures that were the historical remnants of the old Joliet Iron Works. On a late fall rabbit hunt a very strange sight appeared. While approaching an open, grassy area it appeared as if someone had left 20-30 white volleyballs scattered around. Upon closer inspection, the orbs were light in weight, kind of spongy, and had flesh as white as freshly-fallen snow. After carrying one home, my mother identified it as a giant puff-ball mushroom. She sliced and then sautéed part of it in a little butter before letting me taste my first wild mushroom. A week later when hunting in the same field, there was no evidence that they had even been there. It was a mystical mushroom experience.

Another remembrance from rabbit hunting in this area is having the coldest hands possible. It was a morning when the temperature dipped below freezing and there was an abundance of moisture in the air – so much that everything on the ground was covered by heavy hoarfrost. The combination of the damp, cold weather and gripping the cold steel gun barrel caused my hands to hurt. The only thing that would warm me and my hands on a morning like that was to see, shoot, and harvest a plump cottontail. When a pheasant or rabbit was harvested, a messy job of cleaning the game lay ahead. It involved tasks such as gutting, skinning, or plucking – all of which would make a squeamish person retch. It was not enjoyable, but it was my responsibility. The reward for the hunt and the gruesome task of cleaning the game was to sit down to a delicious meal of pan-fried rabbit or pheasant.

Other fall hunts targeted squirrels and doves. The hunting season for this game began in early September when the weather could be absolutely gorgeous. One beautiful fall Saturday morning is forever etched into my memory because of a large wasp. We were hunting along the edge of a large cornfield containing row after row of dried, golden corn stalks. We were hoping to flush a dove as we walked along the edge of the cornfield, but instead chanced upon a cantaloupe vine. The vine had expended all of its energy developing two small melons that we quickly and excitedly harvested. We anticipated the sweet taste of the warm interior as we fruitlessly searched the pockets of our jeans for a knife to cut open the melons. When none was found, we settled on an alternate plan using the top edge of a nearby fencepost to break open the melons. After a few whacks against the post top, the first melon split in two with one half falling to the ground next to the fence post. Immediately, some ground nesting wasps erupted from their nest at the base of the post. Observing one land on my socked ankle caused me to take off running down one of the corn rows as fast as possible to avoid the swarm. Leaves from the stalks and the ears of corn battered me while I sprinted for a good forty yards. Once stopped, I looked down to see that the wasp remained in the same location on my ankle. The only thing that had moved during my forty-yard dash was his abdomen, which shifted up and down in a rhythmic pattern as he repeatedly stung me. Honey bees fall into the "one and done" category, their stingers remaining stuck in your skin. Not so with wasps. My ankle began to swell and by the next day seemed to be the size of the melon I had opened on the fence post.

One of my hunting partners had an older brother who did a lot of duck hunting so three of us decided to try our hand at that. We spent a few Saturdays cutting cattails and other tall grasses to construct a duck blind on the side of the Des Plaines River. Then on the opening day of duck season we carried our guns, and the gunny sacks filled with decoys, for at least two miles in the dark until we reached our blind location. The anticipation of our first duck hunt made the miles seem like blocks. We set up our decoys in the water close to shore and took up our positions in the blind. We watched the sun rise as we listened to and watched the life along the river start a new day. Red-winged blackbirds sang their songs while their feet were firmly clamped to the highest cattails that swayed back and forth in the light breeze. At the same time, muskrats caused wedge-shaped concentric patterns on the calm water's surface as they swam back and forth in the river. Turtles sluggishly pulled themselves from the cool morning river water and up onto dead trees that littered the shallows to soak up the warmth of the rising sun. Frogs called, while looking upward for insects, as we looked skyward for flocks of ducks with ever increasing anticipation. Hours passed without sighting a single duck, so by mid-day we decided to cash it in and pick up the decoys. Then someone noticed some type of a duck swimming close to the opposite shore. A shot was fired, and believing the duck had been hit we walked back to the railroad bridge, in order to cross the river, and then down the opposite river bank to retrieve it. With our prize in hand we celebrated our hunting success. I took it home, where I cleaned and cooked it. It was the worst thing I had ever tasted – it was a coot, not a duck. It tasted like the fish and amphibians it routinely dined on. This, my only duck hunt as a child, as well as all my other hunting experiences, were much the same. We usually returned home completely exhausted and without game in our pouches, yet we always felt like we had just had the time of our lives.

Much like in Minnesota, the winters in Joliet featured snow and freezing temperatures, but they did not keep my friends and me indoors. A nearby natural setting that we called the prison hills is where we headed after any appreciable snowfall. In reality, it was one very large hill that was located on an outlying section of the prison property. This natural feature of the land was the highest point near our neighborhood from which we could launch a snow sled. We called it Thunderbolt Hill because the lightning-fast speed at which we traveled made it scary to go down. Each trip down would induce tears of either fear or joy as we traveled the long run to the bottom. If someone was dislodged from his sled, as it hurled up and over the humps of the terrain, he would flip and flop down the hill like a rag doll until he came to a stop in a crumpled heap. "Boy, that was fun," he would holler, and then immediately begin the grueling ascent of Thunderbolt Hill in order to ride down again.

At the base of the hill was the largest pond we had access to for ice skating and hockey games. This was a natural, spring-fed pond that was considerably larger than the ponds in Heggie hills. Hampering my development as a world-class ice skater was the fact that I never had a pair of skates that were purchased for and actually fit me. Since the loaner or hand-me-down skates were always too large and loose around my ankles, it looked like I was skating on the sides of my ankles. When sides were chosen for a hockey game I was voluntold to be the goalie, due my lack of skating ability and my splayed ankles that helped to deflect the puck. After a few hours of sledding and ice skating in the freezing cold, the only thing guaranteed were nearly frost-bitten feet and hands. The long walk home was followed by the slow removal of ice-crusted clothing. It was amazing how much snow a pair of woolen gloves could retain. If left on the floor to melt, the cat or dog would later be blamed for creating the puddle. After shedding my frozen garments, I would lie, like a cat in a sunny windowsill, on the warm floor next to the furnace register and dream of my daring trips down Thunderbolt Hill. As the snow melted from my woolen gloves and stocking hat, the smell of wet wool filled the air. That unique smell can still transport me back to my childhood.

The realization that enjoying nature was not dependent on a particular location became clear after that first year in Joliet. The outdoor learning experiences, both in Minnesota and in and around Joliet, were a critical part of my childhood education. Direct observation of nature, most often on my own, created in me an interest and desire to understand not just nature, but the broader world around me.

Wait, What are Donuts Made of?

The gift of freedom to explore and learn allowed me to become an independent and optimistic child. As a free-range, baby boomer child, much of my early education was the result of my youthful explorations and at times painful trial and error experiences. Many of these experiences provided a depth of learning way beyond what a parent could explain or teach.

Awareness of the option to watch television rather than explore my neighborhood occurred around the age of three or four. On a bright, sunny, early summer Saturday morning, I was exploring a shady flower garden along the back side of the house. Growing there were these amazing pink flowers that were individually shaped like a heart. They grew on long, curved stems with the pink hearts hanging below in a neat line. While pulling a few of the blossoms off of their stem to dig deeper into their botanical mystery, a delivery truck pulled up to our house. In short order, and to my surprise, our first television was unloaded, uncrated and carried into the house by an installation guy. He then climbed onto the roof of the house and installed the antenna before attaching the wire that lead from it to the television. He switched it on, and for a minute or two, only fuzzy, horizontal lines appeared on the screen while the TV set hissed. Then suddenly and miraculously the Lone Ranger and Tonto appeared galloping across the screen in varying shades of black, gray, and white. As I listened to the Lone Ranger shout, "Hi-ho, Silver," my brain went dormant. This new form of entertainment caused me to temporarily forget the flower garden botanical mystery I had been researching. Getting our first television was an amazing, magical experience that brought joy and wonder right into our house. However, my temporary fascination with television soon took a back seat to exploring the reality that existed all around me. At this young age, it was understood that living a life of doing was more entertaining and fun than watching television.

An abandoned section of pastureland, overgrown with weeds and tall grasses, was the stage for some childhood drama. It was here where, while playing with matches, I started a dry grass fire that required the local volunteer firemen to respond. Matches, and therefore the temptation to play with them, were everywhere because almost every adult smoked cigarettes, including both of my parents. It was fascinating to strike the red tip of a match on the course pad at the bottom of the matchbook and then watch as it magically ignited while emitting an odd-smelling puff of smoke. Friends and I had, in the past, intentionally started small pasture fires and then bravely stamped, like a troupe of Irish step dancers, on the burning grass to extinguish the flames. Experimenting with my friends gave me the courage required to attempt putting out the small fire I had started. But on this occasion, the wind fueled the fire until it was out of my control. Despite my attempts to stamp it out, it grew larger and spread quickly. Panic caused me to flee the scene and run home, with cheeks flush from the heat and anxiety, in clothing smelling of stinky smoke. I quietly entered the house. Hiding in my bedroom, while my heart and mind raced like the passing fire trucks, I listened as the sirens faded into the distance. Later, after creeping from my hiding place, my self-imposed sentence was to spend the balance of the afternoon and evening anxiously awaiting a knock at the door.

My first exposure to fireworks was a painful experiment that went wrong. Around the 4th of July, a group of older neighborhood boys were shooting off bottle rockets and lighting strings of small Black Cat firecrackers. Loud noise, flashes of smoky fire, and the smell of gunpowder attracted us younger boys like a bag of Halloween candy. I watched with fascination as the older boys removed the colorful label and tissue paper that wrapped the firecrackers. Inside were two rows of explosive paper cylinders with their wicks woven together in the center. As they lit the end of the woven wicks with a match, the flame spread up the wicked section and the individual fire crackers began to explode in sequence. This caused me to turn and run back with my hands over my ears to get away from the rapid-fire explosions. Occasionally some of the firecrackers, the duds, would be blown clear of the string of firecrackers without exploding. Younger kids scrambled to pick up these duds as soon as the explosions had ended. They then bent the duds in the middle to break them open, lay them on the ground, and lit the exposed powder with a match. When the powder was ignited, the dud would spin wildly in circles, spewing sparks and smoke, and the kids would attempt to stamp on this rotating sparkler with the heel of a shoe. If they timed it correctly, the spinning cracker would explode and they would cheer at their success. Quickly joining in the search, I almost immediately found a dud. As soon as it was in my hand, with my fingers wrapped securely around it, my clenched fist re-opened at the speed of light while small bits of paper floated toward the ground and smoldering smoke drifted from my stunned hand. I flinched in pain and resisted the urge to cry in front of the other boys, while flexing my fingers to ensure they were still there and in working order. My next step was to quietly retreat to the sidelines to observe the action while continuing to repeatedly flex my tingling fingers. When I lifted my hand closer to my face to look for visible damage, the appealing aroma of burnt gunpowder on my hand triggered me to renew the search for duds.

Trial and error learning also helped me understand how the actions of others could impact me. In a nearby neighbor's yard was a well. The water pump above it caused considerable harm to the index finger on my right hand and forged a lasting memory. It was an upright cast steel pump that had a long, sweeping, curved handle that friends and I pumped up and down to pull water from the well below. We would take turns, individually or in tandem, straining and tugging on the long handle. This allowed each of us to cup our hands under the discharge spout to drink the ice-cold well water. Giggles and hysterical laughing occurred spontaneously when a rushing surge of water ran up one of our noses. At some point, I unknowingly rested the index finger of my right hand in a pinch point near the handle's hinged connection. As someone pulled on the squeaky handle, its downward movement pinched and crushed the tip of my finger. It split open like a banana that had been stepped on. Feeling pain that exceeded anything experienced before led to screams of anguish and tears that flowed down my cheeks to mingle with the well water on my chin. The throbbing pain I felt made the past spankings received for misbehaving seem like acts of affection! Although at this young age swear words were not part of my vocabulary, the rapid succession of loud, distorted sounds that emitted from my contorted mouth could have been interpreted as such. With tears and blood in full flow I ran home to be comforted by my mother who cleaned and bandaged the finger. That night, while trying to sleep, I became aware of the rhythm of my own heartbeat as my aching index finger throbbed in harmony with each beat of my heart.

Each spring, as seasonal thunderstorms rolled into the Midwest, kite kits would appear in the small, mom-and-pop grocery stores that dotted our neighborhood. The act of purchasing a kite kit required optimism and getting one airborne was almost mystical. Before attempting to make the newly-

WAIT, WHAT ARE DONUTS MADE OF?

purchased kite soar into the stratosphere, it had to be assembled into a flying machine. Each kite kit came sealed in a plastic bag that included two long strips of balsa wood and a rolled-up, paper kite with a string inside a pocket that ran around the exterior of the kite. Assembling the kite required me to gently bend the wooden braces so the perimeter string could be inserted into the slots on the ends of the braces. This crucial step sometimes resulted in a broken brace, if over bent, causing my meager collection of swear words to spew from my mouth. If successful, the two braces would form a gently curved, cross-shaped structure at the back of the kite. The next step in this aeronautical engineering exercise was to precisely poke two holes in the paper kite along the length of the longer vertical brace. The holes provided openings so a loop of string could be tied to two connection points on the brace. The end from the spool of string used to hold and control the flying kite was then tied to this loop. The final step was to tie a few strips of a rag to the bottom of the kite. They were intended to provide stability in flight by keeping the kite top facing upward. It was now time to run into the wind and watch the kite soar overhead. To eliminate the risk of electrocution from the power lines that lined all of the streets on the eastside, my friends and I would take our experimental flying machines to Heggie Park for our trial-and-error flight lessons. In the open expanses of Heggie Park, I would hold the kite behind me and run as fast as I could, with the wind in my face, to try and generate enough lift to get the kite airborne. If the wind wasn't strong enough it would be impossible to get the kite up, but that never stopped me from trying. With the paper kite making a fluttering sound behind me, I would continue to run back and forth and to and fro. This effort eventually caused me to fall to the ground, exhausted, while panting like a dog that had been chasing his tail. On ideal, windy kite-flying days, another problem existed. Usually the kites were anything but balanced, so when successful at getting one airborne, the strong winds would cause it to almost immediately go into a death spiral. The wind-driven kite would rotate in an ever-faster circle while spiraling downward until it struck the ground with a loud, quivering thud. Upon impact the whole kite would shudder before the vertical wooden cross brace would explode into splinters. Although the kite was trashed, my ego was only slightly damaged. We all knew trying to get the kite to fly was the real fun. When someone did get one airborne, and stable in the air, they had to stand there like a dork holding a string which quickly led to boredom. By the end of the spring kite-flying season the power lines and trees surrounding Heggie Park were littered with the broken remnants of our kite-flying attempts. Their skeletal remains, though unsightly, had added to our body of knowledge about kite building and flying. We all looked forward to the next kite season with optimism, but not nearly as much as the kite salesman who supplied the neighborhood stores.

The ultimate trial and error sport has to be golf, for the learning never ends. My introduction to golf, the most frustrating sport known to man, happened when someone in our gang of friends starting hitting golf balls in the far corner of Heggie Park. It was natural for the rest of us to want to try this seemingly simple game. To purchase our first golf clubs we went to the appropriate retail outlet – a local antique shop on Collins Street. It was owned by hoarders and as soon as the front door of the shop was opened, an overwhelming, repulsive, dank, musty smell seeped out. This business was on my newspaper route and that unique smell required me to try and hold my breath for five to six minutes when going in to collect payment. By using a combination of rudimentary sign language and grunts, the message to pay up was conveyed. I told my friends that on one occasion, just before turning blue and passing out, some golf clubs had caught my eye in that shop. As we shuffled sideways down the narrow aisles that meandered through the excessive junk we discovered some vintage 1930s wooden-shafted golf clubs. After purchasing clubs, our self-training began in the corner of Heggie Park beyond the baseball diamond outfield. We flailed away at a few used golf balls

WAIT, WHAT ARE DONUTS MADE OF?

and often hit sod divots farther than the ball. Occasionally a flying divot was so large it would block the sun during its overhead spinning flight leading some to believe a flying saucer had passed overhead. This and a lifetime of golf experiences helped me to understand that golf is about enjoying the day and the company, as I could not depend on golf for my fun. Team sports or individual sports played with others, like golf, helped me develop social skills, confidence, and an acceptance of the limits of my abilities. Golf, more specifically, helped me understand that there are rules in life we have to follow. It is also a great ego-limiting game, as no matter how successful or confident I am in life, one round of golf has always managed to humble me.

Almost as much fun as hitting golf balls was the exploratory act of dissecting them to see how they were constructed. Cutting off the white outer cover from a golf ball exposed the inside, which was composed of a small strand of rubber-band-like material that was wound around a small, round rubber ball. Finding and holding the end of the wound material while dropping the tightly wound orb onto the floor caused it to spin and jitter bug around as it unwound itself. Taking things apart to understand their construction was fun.

Practicing almost anything should improve your skills. Board games were a great wintertime activity that helped pass the time and sharpen our mental concentration and problem-solving skills. The mother of all cerebral games was chess. A neighbor kid who was a few years older taught me the game. He needed an opponent to hone his skill set, so he took the time to educate me on the various chess pieces and the rules that governed their movement on the chess board. After a few practice games, to help me get the hang of a game that required some serious mental dexterity, we began to play in earnest. The meaning of "checkmate" quickly became clear as he heartlessly demonstrated his superior skills. This experience taught me that my brain could hurt. I departed for home egoless and that night dreamt of knights, bishops, and pawns. The next day my trial-and-error education continued. My progress was not measured in wins but in the duration of the game. Any game that lasted for more than 10 minutes before he uttered the word checkmate felt like genuine progress. I finally accepted the fact that winning wasn't going to happen anytime soon, and losing over and over again was not that much fun. This game of strategy helped me to develop a strategy of my own. I avoided walking in front of his house for fear of being invited in to play and instead taught one of my younger brothers to play. This allowed me to reconstruct my ego while teaching him the meaning of checkmate.

A school-sponsored science fair project gave me the opportunity to learn via a hands-on experiment. A good friend and I teamed up to both decide upon and then create the required science fair project. We agreed to test the effect of differing diets on study animals. To conduct the actual experiment we purchased two cute, cuddly hamsters and two small cages. They were housed in my dark, scary basement where they could be closely observed and monitored during the defined experiment period. Our plans for the experiment went like this: Hamster number one, may he rest in peace, was fed a balanced diet that contained vegetables and commercially-produced pellets made specifically for hamsters. Hamster number two, may he rest in peace, was fed a mixture of fat, white flour and sugar that had been combined into a pasty, unappetizing lump of junk food. He ate his junk food diet with delight, but after a few weeks visible changes in his appearance and demeanor were observed. He had put on excess weight, his fur coat was disheveled, and he seemed withdrawn and a bit psychotic. While excitingly reporting the findings to my science fair teammate we agreed we had a chance at winning the whole shebang. Then a few nights later when the furnace failed to run during a bitterly cold night, disaster struck. While shivering, I descended the stairs into the very cold basement to feed my little fury friends before departing for school. At first it appeared they were sleeping in, but upon a closer inspection, I discovered they were dead stiff. At school, while in

WAIT, WHAT ARE DONUTS MADE OF?

a stunned and disoriented state, I informed my teammate that the odds of us taking home the trophy were now about as good as the U.S. landing a man on the moon. He drew a bit of attention when he blurted out, "The hamsters died?" By the end of the day we accepted reality and consoled ourselves with the fact that they had given up their lives for science and proceeded to tell their story on our science fair story boards. We could not say, "No animals were harmed in this science experiment," nor did we have any results to report due to the untimely death of our study subjects. We were both so deeply scarred from this experience that we chose careers unrelated to science and pledged to stay away from a diet consisting of only fat mixed with flour and sugar. Wait, what are donuts made of?

Good-intentioned parents at times tried to reduce the risks associated with trial-and-error learning by providing experiential learning opportunities. Early in my high-school years, a new kid moved into the neighborhood. His parents had moved north from southern Illinois where his father had worked at a state prison. He had accepted a position at the nearby Collins Street prison so they picked up, moved, and rented a home not far my mine. The new kid was quickly accepted into our gang of friends. It soon became obvious we were hanging around together for y'all became part of my vocabulary and his mother's delicious biscuits and gravy became my favorite breakfast food. A few months later his father offered to take the two of us on a tour of his workplace. This was long before the "take your child to work" program became popular. Even today it is doubtful that prison employees take their children to work on the "take your child to work" day. Rather than an educational visit, to learn about the ins and outs of the penal system, my friend's father was trying to scare the bejesus out of us – we were about to enter the high-risk age period that involved girls and cars. On the tour, two of our stops were at a laundry and a carpentry shop where the prisoners worked just as if they were on the outside. What really surprised me was that the prisoners all seemed like regular Joes. They had jobs and when they talked with my friend's father it was a respectful conversation both ways. Prison life didn't seem that bad. But then as I looked around it became clear that there were no girls or cars. I quickly put two and two together and left realizing that anyone who lands in prison doesn't have access to girls or cars. Mission accomplished. That was reason enough to behave myself. Not long after that educational field trip, my father gave me a car but didn't offer to teach me how to drive it. Being an independent and optimistic teenager led me to believe that learning to drive could be accomplished by trial-and-error learning.

Nothing symbolized freedom and independence more than getting a driver's license followed by car ownership. In my case the steps were reversed, as car ownership came first. My father gave me his old 1954 Dodge Coronet four-door sedan. It was a relatively ugly two-tone car that was painted a dull, light green over a dull, dark green. Joy and pride filled my heart because it was my first car. Red Ram became its name, for under the hood was a flat-head, six-cylinder engine with the words Red Ram embossed on the head cover. It was in this car that I learned to drive without instructions or help from anyone. My mother did not drive and my father was at the corner tavern. My driving lessons started by cruising around the block in Red Ram and then, over time, slowly expanding my route block by block. Learning to drive is such a powerful memory that I distinctly remember driving on a steamy, hot summer day right after a thunderstorm had rolled through our neighborhood. As the first large drops of rain fell onto the paved road, the smell of summer rain permeated the air. It is hard to describe the smell, but it must have been a combination of steam from the rain hitting the very hot asphalt road surface and the dust kicked up by the rain and wind. Soon after, accompanied by heavy thunder and lightning, it poured cats and dogs for about five minutes. Then, just after the storm passed, the sun broke through the clouds. It was quiet and the air seemed calm and clean. At that precise moment, I slid into the driver's seat and drove around my neighborhood, which seemed deserted since

WAIT, WHAT ARE DONUTS MADE OF?

everyone had taken cover during the storm. This and many more solo sorties developed my confidence to the point that I applied for and received my driver's permit. Within a few weeks, a rather bold decision was made to start driving solo to and from my place of work – a fruit stand. My workplace was only about two miles away and because my route of travel was on quiet neighborhood streets all the way to and from work it felt safe. One day a coworker asked for a ride home. He could quickly see my reluctance to do so because he lived a considerable distance from where we worked. His relentless pestering wore me down and at the end of our workday I agreed. We decided to take a longer route, which would take us through the neighborhoods near my house, rather than drive the more direct path to his house on main thoroughfares. About a half mile into our trip, to my horror, appearing in my rear-view mirror was a police car. The officer may have noticed the sudden look of panic on my face in both the rear view and side mirror. Or maybe he was concerned that the car was driverless due to my 5'5", 125-pound stature. Whatever the reason, he pulled me over, walked up to the car and casually and calmly asked to see my driver's license. Looking up sheepishly, while fumbling through my wallet to get out my permit, I confessed that I didn't have one yet but was driving on a permit. Driving on a permit was permissible if you were accompanied by a licensed driver so he directed his authoritarian glare at my passenger and asked to see his license. My friend squirmed in his seat for a millisecond before quickly blurting out that he didn't have a license. With shaking hands, my coworker opened the car door, said, "I'll see you later," and fled the scene.

After considering his options, the officer asked where I lived and then instructed me to follow him as he led me home. While pulling out onto the roadway and glancing up at the rearview mirror the image of my friend waving from a distance made me feel alone. Sitting in a puddle of sweat and unsure of what would happen next, the Red Ram took its place in the slow, embarrassing, two-car neighborhood parade. After pulling up alongside our house the officer opened his door, went to our front door and knocked until my mother responded. Remaining quietly in the background, while he had a serious discussion with her about the dangers of my actions, seemed the appropriate action. After he pulled away the sentence for my lawlessness was revealed. My car keys were seized by my mother and a two-mile walk to and from work again became the norm.

A few weeks later, after hearing about my run in with the law, a friend who was a licensed driver and owned his own car offered to drive me to the State Driver's License Exam office. My first attempts at completing both the written exam and the road driving test were successful. Very quickly after returning home my mother returned my car keys and driving again replaced walking to and from work. Just a few days later the same friend again asked for a ride home from the fruit stand. This time I agreed without any anxiety or concern. We followed the same exact route we had taken just one week earlier. Police officers were apparently assigned the same patrol area for a period of time because the same officer again observed me driving the green-on-green Dodge Coronet that he had stopped just one week earlier. With his siren blaring and light flashing he pulled up behind the now-stopped "Red Ram." He slowly walked to the driver's side window and gave me a stern look that would have made any parent proud. He surely thought the compassion he had shown a few weeks earlier had been forgotten and he was now prepared to do his duty. He once again asked to see my driver's license and while looking up proudly I handed him my brand-spanking-new license. We were both happy with the outcome, for he had an almost imperceptible smile on his face as he handed back my license. He had used his authority to direct me down the right path. Life is good when you do the right things guided by people who care.

Not long after this experience a friend decided he was going to teach one of my younger sisters, with whom he may have been enamored, how to drive a stick shift vehicle. He owned a brand new, high-powered Plymouth muscle car that had the horsepower equivalent of a teenage boy's testosterone levels. A driver's lesson like that is best given in a large parking lot with other vehicles no closer than a quarter mile. But for some reason he chose to begin her driver's education right next to our house with his car parked directly in front of mine. The main challenge when learning to drive a manual stick shift car is to maintain the delicate balance between clutch engagement and gas flow to the engine. Too much clutch, too fast, can cause the car to lurch forward like a bucking bronco and the rear wheels to spin. Not enough clutch engagement can cause the car to stall abruptly. Surely he used this universally accepted phrase to instruct her – "Let out the clutch pedal slowly, while at the same time give the car a little gas." Getting that combination right on the first try is nearly impossible because you only learn what "slowly" and "little" mean through experience. It's like trying to tell someone how hard to hold a cat before dunking it into a tub of water for a bath. Her first attempt caused the high-horsepower Mopar to quickly and suddenly lurch. The big surprise to all was the direction of the lurch, for the car was in reverse rather than first. This was before head rests were standard in cars so they both had a great view of the dome light for a fraction of a second as their heads jerked back upon impact with my car. Luckily, it was my first car – the old "Red Ram" – which was a tank of a car, that took the hit. In 1954 when it was built, gas sold for around 23 cents per gallon and most cars were akin to military tanks. The oil crisis of 1973-74, which saw oil prices skyrocket from $2.00 to $6.00 per barrel, drove an interest in smaller, fuel-efficient vehicles. But in 1954 the words "fuel" and "economy" had not yet been used together in the same sentence! No real harm was done to my car, but within six months a newer car replaced the Red Ram.

My second car was a baby blue, 1955 Ford 2-door sedan, which provided new learning opportunities. To finance the purchase, I sold the Red Ram to someone who was desperately in need of transportation. Being a 2-door rather than a 4-door vehicle automatically made the Ford a better or at least better-looking car. Very quickly after the purchase, the euphoria of new car ownership stalled when it was revealed that the car had some engine issues. A plume of baby-blue smoke followed my baby-blue Ford wherever it went. It was an oil burner. If the wind direction was from the rear, when stopped at a red light the smoke would shroud the car and cause me to hold my breath for a minute. Despite the neighborhood mosquito reduction benefits the car provided, a search for a repair garage to assess the situation ensued. After inspecting the car, the mechanic concluded it needed to have the piston rings replaced. A lot of hard-earned money later, the car no longer burned oil, but it was now very difficult to start. Of course, the mechanics said they were certain the engine repairs they had completed were unrelated to the starting problem. This was problematic for me for I was unfamiliar with engine repairs but remembered my car started fine before the repairs. Although angry at the situation, I tried to live with this difficult car, but ultimately the relationship was untenable. The solution was to purchase another used car and sell off the baby-blue Ford. The new owner was excited when he was informed the car had just had the piston rings replaced. Seeing his excitement combined with my now considerable experience at buying and selling vehicles tempted me to consider used car sales as a career. Then I realized that choice might entail lying to people daily.

The car you owned said a lot about who you were – or at least we believed that as teenagers. We all thought if we just had the right car, girls would climb into the back seat to make out without even being asked! My newest auto acquisition had some real class and style. It was a '57 Ford Fairlane convertible that had undergone a bit of customization work that made it a cool car to own and drive. It had metallic silver paint, a custom black interior, Hurst four-speed on the floor, and a 351-cubic-inch V-8 interceptor engine. This was my first stick shift transmission car and, after mastering the art of using a clutch, it was fun to drive. Spinning the rear tires intentionally, when taking off from a dead

WAIT, WHAT ARE DONUTS MADE OF?

stop, by popping the clutch resulted in the squeal of the tires and the smell of burnt rubber, which were appealing to a seventeen-year-old. Girls were also appealing, but even though I now owned a cool car, I still had not been on a real date.

My first real date occurred when I attended my high-school senior prom. A friend asked if I would like to go with his girlfriend's friend. Although we had never met, it was agreed we would be the blind-date couple on a double date for prom night. Renting a tuxedo and ordering flowers in preparation for the big night resulted in a new type of excitement. Like all teenage boys who dreamt about dating, without knowing what that entailed, I anticipated a night of new experiences and exploration. When prom day arrived, my friend arrived at my house in his father's new Chrysler. After picking up his date, we proceeded to my date's house. Apprehensively, I approached her front door, knocked, and was invited in by her parents. They observed a nervous teenage boy gawking at their daughter as she made her entrance in a beautiful gown. With sweaty hands, the corsage was passed from me to my date, and then to her mother, who helped pin the floral arrangement onto her gown. Within minutes we were in the back seat of the Chrysler and driven to a steakhouse for a pre-prom dinner. After settling the bill, which entailed shelling out more money for a meal than ever before, we drove to the prom location for a night of dancing, fun, and who knows what else. The anticipation of what might occur that prom night turned out to be much better than what actually occurred. Before the night ended and we dropped my date off at her home, I felt like a vehicle, much like the new Chrysler, used simply to transport my date to the dance and her friends. At the dance she spent more time with her girlfriends than with me. Realizing a blind date could simply be someone's ticket into the prom left me feeling odd and out of place. Back at her house I walked her to the front door and simply said goodnight. Later, while lying in bed unable to sleep, it became clear that both the positive and the negative of dating was the intense feeling of tension and anxiety. The awkwardness of the evening was due to my lack of dating experience. My optimistic outlook allowed me to believe my dating experiences would improve because of my understanding of the trial-and-error learning process. I accepted and learned from all my experiences, good and bad, and then quickly moved on with life. A few weeks later the prom photo taken at the dance arrived in the mail. I opened the envelope and stared at the photo of me standing next to a total stranger who had taught me my first lessons about dating.

One activity, cooking, was the perfect experience to teach me about optimistic trial-and-error learning and creativity. From an early age, I fed my interest in exploring the world of food by spending time in the kitchen. Because of my insatiable craving for sweets, my earliest kitchen endeavors were candy making. Anyone who has ever made candy understands that it is a finicky and troublesome cooking process, which is why many of my early attempts ended in utter disappointment. Unaware of the almost-certain failure ahead, a recipe would be selected and the ingredients gathered to make penuche, brown-sugar fudge, or traditional chocolate fudge. Then, on a Sunday afternoon, in between dashes into the living room to view bits of Mutual of Omaha's Wild Kingdom or Victory at Sea, the boiling candy would scent the kitchen with the smell of sugary goodness. My desire to make penuche was driven by my love of a confection sold under the name "Coconut Haystacks." Sitting on a white, pressed-board base, and sealed in a cellophane wrapper were four small mounds of delicious brown-sugar fudge that had been combined with shredded coconut. My many failures at candy making could be divided into two distinct categories. Either the candy did not set up and remained a runny mess or the candy crystalized into a rock-hard, inedible mass. Candy making requires boiling the sugar syrup to an exact temperature. A thermometer to gauge the temperature was unavailable, but an alternate method described in a cookbook helped me decide when to stop boiling the syrup. The technique required me to drop a small amount of the hot syrup into cold water and then pick up and gently squeeze the glob of sugar to determine if it had reached the requisite "soft-ball stage." My attempts provided candy-making experience, but rarely the chance to taste the creamy goodness of a properly made piece of fudge. I persevered and began to understand that if candy making was easy, everyone would make his or her own. Anything we attempt in life that is difficult brings added pleasure, and sometimes sweetness, when we are successful.

Learning on your own, because you have an interest in something, is a very different learning experience when compared to being told what to do and how to do it, as in high school. Doing just enough work to get by in high school meant I was an average student. All English and math classes were pretty much the same; they just got more difficult as the material taught became more complex. Science classes, on the other hand, offered me some new learning. My biology teacher was a knowledgeable, kind, easy-going, and compassionate lay teacher. He made both the class and learning fun, which, when combined with my interest in nature, meant my grades were respectable. He focused us on learning by doing; experiential learning that engaged us in the learning process. As a result, dissecting small animals and the smell of formaldehyde actually appealed to me. Then the following year, chemistry appeared on my schedule of classes. The instructor was an uncaring, pretentious, almost-arrogant priest who believed rote memorization was the key to success. He did not want to engage and teach students, he wanted to direct them. The periodic table was my downfall. My hopes of conducting endless, hands-on experiments using the Bunsen burner that was right in front of me on the lab table, rather than memorize the symbols and names of the elements listed on the periodic table, were dashed. Clogging my brain with facts that were available on a chart was what he expected of me. My interest in him and the subject quickly waned, which allowed him to exercise his right to fail me in the second semester of chemistry. One thing he did teach me is that failure is part of life and that it is okay. School exposes us to many subjects that will help us find our true path, and chemistry was not located on mine.

My Spanish teacher had, and taught me about, an "attitude." He was a lay teacher of short stature who seemed to believe his height entitled him to fully exercise the traits of someone with a Napoleon complex. Everyone in the class thought "Senor" was from Mexico because of his accent, olive complexion, black hair and the fact that he spoke Spanish as his first language. We were not very worldly and never even considered the fact that someone from Spain could be teaching us Spanish. Any misconception about his country of origin was quickly clarified if someone made the mistake of implying he was Mexican. This suggestion caused him to flare up like a miniature volcano and spew the words, "I am from Spain; I am Spanish, not Mexican!" Even though we envisioned him in a serape and sandals, he wore a dark suit every day and walked around like a banty rooster. He was a man proud of his Spanish heritage and we used that to our advantage. We could always direct him off of the subject being discussed in class by asking him questions about life in Spain. "Senior, qué comen en España?"

My math classes were challenging enough that they taught me how to struggle through a class. Sitting and stressing over my math homework was a nightly occurrence. It never came easy to me. After completing geometry and two years of algebra, the school staff must have looked at my performance in chemistry and decided to give me a pass when it came to calculus. My geometry instructor was a fun-spirited priest who had a red, ruddy complexion that may have been linked to the beer truck that stopped in front of the school every few weeks. From his classroom windows, we would observe the truck pull up and then watch the driver load multiple cases of beer onto his hand truck before delivering them to the rectory next to the school. Someone noted he once observed this teacher licking his lips when the delivery truck arrived.

WAIT, WHAT ARE DONUTS MADE OF?

The structured learning provided in school helped prepare me for the adult level decision making that would soon be required. For instance, entering the military was a unique learning experience that taught me some life lessons. While enlisting, my recruiter opened a binder that listed all of the possible entry-level air force job descriptions and asked me what type of work interested me. Believing there would be work available in this field after my discharge, my first, second, and third choices, which were recorded on the official form, had to do with the field of photography. An interest in photography had developed from my exposure to a friend who had his own home darkroom. As the recruiter read through my choices he cautioned me that there was no guarantee of getting my first choice. After completing basic training and departing for my first duty station, it became clear that what the recruiter promised or what you had written on the form was meaningless. My orders noted my training would be to become a Fuels Specialist while assigned to the POL (Petroleum, Oil, and Lubricants) unit at an airbase in northern Louisiana. In the military, what you want is secondary to what they need. This assignment reinforced what I instinctively already knew – the work culture in the military did not appeal to me. I wanted to be in charge of my own life. That line of thinking was reinforced during my last week of basic training when we were informed we were to be given squadron leave for an afternoon. This meant no training and an opportunity to leave the barracks and walk to the Base Exchange, a store where soft drinks and snacks could be purchased. While approaching the exchange, we had to walk around a flight of airmen standing in formation on the sidewalk. As we came around the other side of the recruits, their drill instructor screamed out, "Airman, what are you doing walking on the grass?" We said, "yes, sir" and, "no, sir" to him as we explained the obvious – the sidewalk was blocked by the flight of recruits. Noteworthy, and obvious to us, was that this was an almost-desert terrain where there was no grass! He chewed our butts and then asked for both our flight number and the name of our drill instructor. When we returned to our barracks our drill instructor was waiting for us. After some more butt chewing he informed us we were restricted to the barracks for the balance of basic training since we had been disrespectful to the other drill instructor. As he repeated what he had been told, it was obvious he had been lied to. Having to accept that someone could lie about what had occurred while only being able to respond with, "yes, sir" and, "sorry, sir," was a revelation. During my four years in the Air Force the importance and timeliness of that situation was often recalled. Three weeks into my four-year enlistment, getting out became my objective and I never considered reenlistment. Life is one long learning experience, and that situation helped me understand that a work culture is more important than the type of work performed.

Size Matters

"Runt" might have been an appropriate nickname for me during high school. I was one of the shortest students and weighed 135 pounds when I graduated. During my four years in the U.S. Air Force, a growth spurt finally occurred. Six inches in height and twenty pounds of body weight changed my appearance. Two years after my discharge from the military, long, hippy hair and a beard, in combination with the changes in my physical appearance, made me a mystery guest at my five-year high-school reunion. "Who is that?" was whispered over and over as I passed former classmates who only remembered the short, skinny me. By this time, I was in my early twenties and I had long before accepted me as I was.

Despite my small stature, I played all types of sports with my friends while growing up. Most of these games took place at Heggie Park, which was just a block from home. The park had just one ball diamond, which was usually available during the day. In the searing summer heat of mid-day, my gang of friends would meet on the dusty diamond, choose sides, and play ball until late afternoon when the park groundskeeper would chase us from the field. He would then rake around the bases and mound, water the infield, and then chalk the base lines and batter's box using a bright white, chalky substance. This same grumpy groundskeeper, who had a complexion that was a ruddy, weathered red, was known to be fond of Muscatel wine, which came in clear, flat, glass pint bottles. The wine was a bright, almost piss-colored yellow liquid. I am not sure if it is true, and let's hope it is not, but a story circulated that someone may have peed in an empty wine bottle and left it in the field house where the groundkeeper stored his things. His late afternoon field work was to prepare the diamond for the adult leagues that would play in the evening. The adult fast-pitch softball league had pitchers who would deliver on target pitches at a velocity of over 50 mph by rotating their arms in a windmill, circular fashion before releasing the ball. One pitcher in particular, a tall, lanky individual, would cause me to stay and endure the ever-present hordes of mosquitos drawn to the diamond by the overhead field lights, because he was so good. I appreciated him and other talented athletes because of my lack of athletic ability.

We frequently played ball and when young we only played hard ball. As we and our hands grew, we also played 12" softball and another game unique to the Chicago area – 16" softball. Trying to throw and catch this mushy, large ball was quite challenging for someone of my small stature. When a fly ball was hit in my direction, my instincts were to run in the opposite direction to avoid the large projectile falling from the sky. If my hand alignment was just slightly off and the ball hit only my fingertips it could bend back and dislocate multiple fingers simultaneously. That thought caused me to flee, while shouting to my teammates, "I almost had it!"

Size matters in most sports and I didn't have it. My sports ego was as undersized as my stature. All my friends understood my team sports contribution was limited to filling an open position so the game could be played. Being selected for a baseball team caused me to automatically run to right field to take up my position. When basketball sides were chosen, one of the last selected for a side would be me and some of the earlier picks for my team might still groan at the choice. It was understood I wouldn't be shooting the ball on offense. My accepted role was to make a nuisance of myself on defense by relentlessly dogging whomever had the ball. It was extremely frustrating for them and rewarding for me. I felt like I was making a difference in my own way and began to understand, and more importantly accept, not everyone can be the star of the team. Using the little talent I had to make a difference made me feel good about my contribution. My parents never watched me play sports. No one encouraged me or helped me get through the disappointments and defeats that are part of sports. Coping with my lack of ability was my burden; I internalized it and learned from it. I learned to accept me.

When baseball season ended, we would meet on cool fall days and choose sides for football games. It didn't matter if we played touch or tackle football; my time was spent trying to avoid everyone, no matter what team they were on, to avoid personal injury. My lack of desire to throw my body in front of running friends seemed normal to me. Another factor that stymied the growth of my athletic ability and confidence was the fact that a week after graduating from grade school I contracted Rheumatic Fever. That occurrence not only prevented me from playing sports, it wrecked my summer!

While walking my paper route one day, noticeable pain was felt in my knees. Within a few days it was severe enough that I couldn't or didn't want to walk because of the pain. My mother called my namesake, Uncle Bob, who worked shift work and was home at the time, and he transported us to the local hospital. The diagnosis was Rheumatic Fever, which resulted in me spending the first three weeks of summer vacation in the hospital and much of the balance of the summer on the living room couch. It was a lonesome period for me. The hospital had limited visitation hours for adults and children were never allowed in the hospital to visit family or friends. This decades-old hospital was constructed in multiple building additions over the years, so some sections were higher than others. The window of my room looked out over the graveled roof of an adjoining section which, because it was built into a hillside, had a very low wall that faced the hill. While peering out my window, a mirage caused by the heat rising from the hot, white, graveled roof had me imagining people walking across the roof. Rubbing my eyes and looking again produced images of my friends. The voices of my childhood friends were as unmistakable as those of my parents. Just observing their approach and hearing their voices lifted my spirits. They explained that since they were denied entry by the hospital staff, they decided to climb onto the roof to visit me through my open window. Their act of kindness helped me understand friendship on a new level. Following my discharge the doctor instructed me to take it easy and not do much of anything. That translated to lying on our couch or limping to Heggie Park to watch my friends play sports and horse around. When young, each day, each week, and indeed the whole summer seemed to last forever. This summer lasted an eternity. I was happy when the school year began. My doctor recommended that I not take gym class that first semester of high school to allow my joints additional time to heal. The request for a schedule change was submitted and approved. As a result, the one benefit of having contracted Rheumatic Fever was no gym class! For the subsequent seven semesters, when sitting down with my counselor to select my classes for the upcoming term, I sadly (wink, wink) informed him of my medical restriction. Consequently, any athletic development that might have occurred during my high school years was squandered by yours truly.

    I was a very sensitive child but tried my best to not outwardly display my emotions. Although most often successful, on one occasion red, teary eyes revealed my secret. With my gang of friends on Saturday mornings, we would walk 30 minutes down Collins Street, with our heel cleats clickety-clacking, on our way to the city center and the Rialto Theater – a massive, glamorous vaudeville-era theater that opened in 1926. The theatre entrance featured huge marble columns and dual winding stairways that led to the balcony seating. On my first visit I looked around in wide-eyed wonderment. It seemed like a movie set. Every Saturday morning, the popcorn-scented theatre would attract kids from all over Joliet by showing a double feature of children's movies. Before going to the theater we would pick up our discounted movie supplies by stopping at a large variety store to purchase a long paper tube of fresh popcorn or at a corner drug store for candy that would sustain us through the opening cartoons and two full-length movies. Wearing a jacket to the movies, no matter what the temperature outside, allowed me to jam the tube of popcorn into a sleeve and fill the pockets with a few of my favorite candy bars like the Butterfinger, Clark bar, Babe Ruth or the exotic-sounding English toffee Heath bar. On one Saturday morning, I fell in love with the Cadbury milk chocolate bar smuggled into the theatre. It was from far-away England and had a creamy, chocolatey taste with caramel overtones that helped me to understand and appreciate that not all chocolate came from or tasted like Hershey's.

Featured each Saturday were a variety of funny, scary, and even sad movies. One Saturday morning found me eating soggy popcorn that had been dampened by my tears. During the Walt Disney tear-jerker *Old Yeller*, a dog – not just any dog, but the star of the movie – is put down because it was believed he had contracted rabies. Still healing from the trauma of having to leave my Irish Setter Sparky in Minnesota caused me to sympathize with the boy who was about to have his dog murdered on the big screen. The darkness of the theatre hid the tears welling up and then flowing freely from my eyes. When the lights were turned on my friends saw my red eyes and accused me of crying in the movie. A story was quickly concocted about someone throwing a Jujube, those hard little candies that were only good for throwing in the theater, and it had hit me in one eye, ricocheted off of a seat back and then hit my other eye. It was a white lie that they did not buy.

Movies were powerful, educational, and entertaining experiences. When the movie *The Ten Commandments* was playing at the Rialto, our grade school teacher, the nun, strongly encouraged us to individually see the movie. Apparently, it wasn't Catholic enough for a field trip to be organized. When I arrived, there was a line of people waiting to get into the lobby to purchase a ticket. The movie had a plot line that was well documented and widely understood, yet the line circled around the corner and down a side street. With ticket in hand I found one of the few remaining seats in the jam-packed theatre just in time to view a movie spectacle unlike any I had seen before. When Moses parted the waters to allow his people to pass just before soldiers and horse draw chariots were swept away in the collapsing walls of water, it was pure movie magic on a grand scale. While watching, my eyes must have been as big as Nefertiti's – without the eye makeup of course. It wasn't the story line that impressed me, but rather the technical movie magic. The director had created something that pulled me into the large, Technicolor landscape and I temporarily escaped from the realities of life.

Another movie that intrigued me was the 007 spy thriller titled, *Goldfinger*. The film score playing on the stereo theater sound system just blew me away. While the opening credits were rolling, Shirley Bassey sang the title song in a vibrant, strong voice. Her performance was followed by a fast-paced, action-filled movie with characters that had strange but intriguing names like Oddjob and Pussy Galore. Movies were magic.

Being short, sensitive, and shy didn't help me when I first began to take notice of and have an interest in girls. At this time "interest" was defined as looking at them from afar. The opposite sex was as mysterious as a distant galaxy full of twinkling stars to a teenager who attended an all-boys high school. Like the stars, they were visible, but personal knowledge or understanding of their inner workings was non-existent. The only girls around were my sisters or those who lived in my neighborhood. Gaining access to a larger selection of girls, while furthering my sex education, was accomplished by attending weekend dances sponsored by two different schools. Both were revenue-generating events that featuring recorded, or on some occasions, live music. The first venue was my high school and the second was a Catholic grade school on the near-west side of Joliet. Many of the teachers at my high school were priests or religious brothers. Just prior to the Sunday night dance, they stationed themselves at the dance entrance so they could play the role of the anti-sex police force. They monitored us as we paid the entrance fee to ensure we were wearing appropriate clothing. They entertained themselves by making sarcastic comments like, "Were you poured into those jeans, or were they tattooed on?" This was their way of letting us know that tight clothing would lead to loose morals and eventual eternal damnation in hell. Then during the dance, they would roam around the dance floor looking for any opposite-sex body parts that might come into inappropriate contact. If any of us was lucky enough to find a girl who would slow dance with us, we attracted priests and brothers like shoppers to a blue-light special at K-Mart. They would swarm to the pending warmth, with a flashlight in hand to ensure light would shine between the dancers, in order to extinguish the glow. At both dance venues, groups of boys and girls would gather like herds of grazing animals on the savannahs of Africa. The zebras and the wildebeests kept to themselves and rarely co-mingled. The boys clowned around while trying to act cool as the girls talking incessantly and nervously about the "cute boys." These clusters of girls and boys would almost imperceptibly move around the dance floor like giant, pulsating amoebas that were always in flux and full of nervous energy. Success at getting a girl to dance with you, followed in succession by dating, making out, getting to first and then all of the other bases and eventually marriage, was all based on the courage one possessed. Being a slight boy who lacked confidence and courage meant a lot of looking but very little asking. Asking someone to dance and getting refused was a crushing blow to my slight teenage ego. To help prevent this physiological damage, showcasing my dancing skills while dancing in a circle with a cluster of boys and girls was always a safe way to entertain myself. We would laugh and gyrate while dancing to *Wooly Bully* by Sam the Sham and the Pharaohs. It was a song with a great beat that, because of the lyrics, helped us all learn to count to four in Spanish. "Uno, dos, one, two, tres, cuatro / Matty told Hatty about a thing she saw / Had two big horns and a wooly jaw / Wooly bully, wooly bully..."

Occasionally during the night, to signal a slow dance, the lights would dim, which caused me to retreat to the sidelines; asking a girl to dance was too frightening. Most of the boys, including me, stood around wishing and hoping we had a dance partner. When Bobby Vinton sang *Mr. Lonely* we all thought the song had been written especially for us. "Lonely, I'm Mr. Lonely, I have nobody for my own, I am so lonely, I'm Mr. Lonely, wish I had someone to call on the phone...." The few boys who possessed big egos and loads of confidence seemed to always be dancing with the pretty girls while most of us were dancing in circles with friends. Despite the fact that my lack of confidence kept me from closely interacting with the girls, I learned to love music and dancing, which brought joy to my life.

At some point, despite my stature, I had to grow up. This type of growing up had nothing to do with my physical size and everything to do with accepting responsibility for my actions. Young children are often told to "act their age" by their parents. Personally defining what that meant, while in a particular situation and then deciding how to act or react, was the process of growing up. My large family situation and my parents' preoccupation with other things meant I was rarely given specific advice or direction and therefore felt a sense of freedom to explore and learn by doing.

Where to go, what to do, and whom to do it with were daily questions for boys like me who were afforded the freedom to explore and learn. The answer to where to go was often Heggie Park or Heggie hills. One of the most important features of my Joliet neighborhood was Heggie Park, which was located just one block from my home. In size the park was equivalent to a half city block. Just north of the park was a large, old industrial building that in its heyday was home to the Heggie Manufacturing Company, a producer of boilers. The park, which was named after the company's founder, James Heggie, contained a baseball field, a pavilion, tennis courts, and a basketball court. During the summer, the park district hired young college students to facilitate the different activities at Heggie Park. They included arts and crafts projects, field trips, sports, and even a pet contest. Two of my cousins entered their dog Loraine into the pet contest and she won the top prize. Loraine was a sweet, gentle, Border collie mix who didn't mind me being part of her pack for the ribbon presentation photo. We were certainly excited a few days later when a picture featuring Loraine sitting in front of the three of us appeared in the local newspaper. The park district was responsible for my first trips into the big city of Chicago, and they were memorable events. I attended two park-district-sponsored field trips to Chicago's major league baseball parks – Comiskey Park, home of the Chicago White Sox, as well as Wrigley Field, home of the Chicago Cubs. The trip to Comiskey sticks in my mind because the park was an enormous place. It was a bright, sunny day and the hum of the large crowd was a noise new to me. When a White Sox batter made contact with the ball, the crack of the bat echoed around the field, followed by thunderous clapping. Of course, as a young child my short attention span wouldn't allow me to sit in my bleacher seat and watch the entire game. So instead I walked around the stadium and at one point felt really lost and wasn't sure how to get back to my seat. Luckily an usher recognized my look of worry, or the tears welling up in my eyes, and helped me route my return path.

I also recall a park-district-sponsored trip to a very large amusement park in Chicago called Riverview Park. It was 74 acres of fun for most people, but for me it was 74 acres of stomach pain and nausea. The Comet, Silver Flash, Fireball, and the Bobs were all roller coasters that would have sickened me, yet thrilled thousands of attendees from 1904 until 1967, when the park closed. I spent my day and my meager funds eating delicacies like cotton candy and corn dogs while playing arcade games and watching others, who had the stomachs for it, ride the many roller coasters. Their fear-inducing screams echoed throughout the park non-stop and helped to ensure I never summoned up the courage to get in line for a roller coaster ride.

Heggie hills was an old, overgrown industrial wasteland that was adjacent to the park. During the spring, summer, fall, and winter the park and the hills were the equivalent of Mecca, the Wailing Wall, Lumbini, and the Vatican to me and my friends. If we weren't at home or in the park, we were probably in the hills. No matter how much fun was afforded us at Heggie Park, it paled in comparison to our exploits and explorations in Heggie hills. This was our secret meeting place where we entertained ourselves, including doing some things we weren't supposed to do.

In the fall, when the wild grasses and weedy plants of Heggie hills turned from an assortment of greens into various shades of browns and tans, we would instigate an extensive search of the whole neighborhood for large, empty, corrugated boxes. A good, flattened corrugated box on dry grass was as slick as a sled's runners on icy snow. We would haul our corrugated sleds to the highest hill and while hanging onto the upturned front edge of the flattened box, push off and rocket down the grassy slope. Of course the slopes contained more than just grass, which resulted in some bruising of our behinds. When you sled on snow the layer of snow along with the sled protects your rear end from any protruding rocks and debris. On cardboard it was a rough, ass-bruising ride. On one occasion, in between trips down the hill, someone came up with the brilliant idea to use some broken pieces of a mirror we had found to signal, or temporarily blind, each other using the sun as the light source. We quickly tired of that activity and all headed up the hill for another trip down. My cousin, who had found a really nice chunk of mirror, decided to put it in his pocket for safe keeping while he took his next ride down the grass toboggan slide. After his trip to the bottom of the hill he was delighted to find that his signaling mirror was still intact, but somewhat dismayed that the mirror had sliced open not only his pants, but also his thigh. A ghastly gash that was about an inch deep and two inches long caused all of our eyes to widen to that same approximate size when he dropped his trousers to display the wound. Even before thinking about treating the wound, we began the ever-important dialogue concerning how he was going to "explain this to his mother." We settled on a story about him tripping and falling onto a piece of glass. We helped him home and then everyone except me ran in different directions to avoid involvement. I stuck around, watching through squinted eyes as he poured hydrogen peroxide on the deep wound to disinfect it. I felt like fainting as he murmured like a girl when the disinfectant hit the open wound and bubbled like a 7-Up being poured into a glass that contained a little blood. Stitches at the local hospital sealed the wound, while the truth about what really happened stayed sealed behind our gang's lips – for at least a day.

This wasn't the only time my cousin was injured in the hills. When parents everywhere tell children "you'll shoot your eye out" when they ask for a BB gun, they must know it is a real possibility. Thank goodness nobody lost an eye in Heggie hills. But if a group of pre-teens are all armed with BB guns, there is likely to be some damage that occurs. So just as when sides were selected for a pick-up baseball or basketball game, sides were selected for a BB gun war. Now, of course there were rules to prevent injuries. Everyone's head nodded in agreement, like bobble-head dolls, when someone suggested we not aim at each other's heads. After all, we had all heard a lecture including "you'll shoot your eye out" when we begged for and were given our guns. The problem with a rule like that is when fighting skirmishes in Heggie hills, we were most often lying down and peering over a hill or bush and only our head, arms and weapon were exposed. There was also a very big assumption that everyone could shoot straight with a low-powered BB gun known for its inability to shoot straight. The good news is that my cousin did not have to go back to the hospital – this time it was the dentist. Someone, whom I am sure was aiming well below my cousin's head, sent a BB flying that broke one of his front teeth in half. We immediately concocted a plan requiring him to not smile for the balance of his life so that no one would notice his tooth. As a back-up plan we agreed he had tripped and fallen on a rock, thus breaking his tooth. We were concerned that his mother might notice the trend of tripping accident stories, but it was the best lie we could summon up while under pressure.

The hills also hid some of our secrets. When it was time for us to try smoking cigarettes, as many children did and do, this is where it happened. We pooled our meager financial resources and someone wandered confidently into a small grocery store near his home and bought a pack of smokes for one of "[his] parents." Once the score had been made, we met in the hills and while acting cool, smoked one cigarette after another until the pack was empty, to ensure there was no evidence left. Before heading home, the cigarette smell had to be purged from my mouth. Gum – Juicy Fruit or Doublemint – was the first choice, and if it was unavailable, we relied on chewing a handful of chlorophyll-filled blades of grass. It didn't taste very good but we believed it did the job. Later if my mother were to ask, "What is that green stuff stuck in your teeth?" I would simply and calmly say I had eaten a salad at a friend's house. Oh, and I had blue cheese dressing!

Today the internet, television, and the movies provide more opportunities to observe the opposite sex scantily clad than we had chances to look at girls fully dressed. Most all of us went to Catholic grade schools where the nuns had instilled, or beat into us, a strong sense of right and wrong – especially when it came to anything sexual. I wasn't even sure if I was supposed to look at the girls in my class unless I raised my hand and asked for permission. Someone, somewhere, maybe in his dad's sock drawer, came across a few copies of some very dated girly pin-up magazines and brought a small stash of them to the hills. They weren't as graphic as a Playboy magazine but they still revealed sights we hadn't even dreamt of or knew existed. My friends and I all had a good look and then walked home very slowly, either limping or bow legged.

All teenage boys eventually experiment with alcohol and my gang of friends was no different. As we found and worked better-paying jobs, and the reward of car ownership became the norm, the pursuit of illegally purchased alcoholic beverages was an allure almost equal to the pursuit of girls. Older brothers and drunks on the street all became potential buyers. Out-of-the-way taverns located in the least desirable parts of town were our favorite suppliers. Beer was the beverage of choice for my friends, which made it easy for me to "just say no" to drinking, for the taste of beer had no appeal. My dislike was somehow related to the fact that my father drank beer every day and I was stubbornly determined to be different. All of the experimentation we did together helped me to grow, not in stature, but in my ability to recognize and make adult decisions. Learning to speak up and say no rather than be pressured by others to do things was a sign of real growth. Feeling a sense of independence and optimism made it easier to transition from a being a teen to an adult.

When I graduated from high school in 1964, the military draft was in place and it was the pipeline used by the government to supply troops for the Vietnam War. Since I went to work at U.S. Steel immediately after graduating high school, rather than attend college, within a few months of my graduation, a notice from the local draft board arrived in the mail. Standing in the kitchen and opening that letter with quivering hands was a sobering experience that expedited the realization that my childhood was ending. There was not yet a draft lottery based on birth dates and without a college deferment, which at that time kept a person from being drafted until after their college graduation, I was singled out as someone who was ready to serve his country. My passing that preliminary physical was an early indicator that the Vietnam jungle and an M-16 assault rifle could be in my very near future. Confronting the reality of going into a war zone to kill or be killed scared the shit out of me and forced me to make my first real adult decision.

My physical stature, 5 foot 6 inches tall and 135 pounds, made it difficult to envision myself as a ground soldier in Vietnam. The draft board, the military, and I all understood there was an opportunity to make a personal choice to serve my country rather than be drafted and forced into the military. Joining the military was a thought that had never entered my mind before this point in time. Now with the likelihood of me being drafted the decision to explore enlisting, which meant serving three to four years in the military, versus two if drafted, was made. The military recruitment offices were in downtown Joliet and visiting them was my next step. Although there were four choices, as all branches of the military had representatives in the recruiting office, there was really only one option. Joining the U.S Army made no sense, as that might result in me becoming a ground soldier in the jungles of Vietnam – the very situation I was trying to avoid. Enlisting in the Marines seemed like a form of suicide to me. My personality and that of a marine seemed to be on the opposite ends of the aggression spectrum. Joining the Navy was also out of the question. Not knowing how to swim and my childhood experience on the tilt-a-whirl helped me to understand that my pre-disposition to motion sickness might have me puking for four years while riding the high seas. Despite the Navy recruiter's assurance that it would "be okay," my stomach hurt thinking about the prospect and I left to talk to my last option – the Air Force recruiter. He of course was very happy to see me, for he had a monthly quota to meet. He told me all the things a potential recruit wants to hear. Once trained in a field of my choice, my four years of service would fly by as quickly as the jet planes making bombing runs in Vietnam. I weighed my options without input from my parents or anyone else. I realized a Vietnam assignment while in the Air Force was still a possibility, but as least it would be on an airbase rather than in the jungle. The unknown future seemed a much better option than my potential death in Vietnam, so the decision to join the U.S Air Force was made. My recruiter offered, and I agreed to, a delayed enlistment, which was the organization's way of load leveling the recruits being sent to basic training. This meant my enlistment was confirmed but my departure for basic training would be delayed a few months. Life and work continued as if everything was normal but as the days and weeks passed I began to prepare for my departure. I sold my car, gave away my guitar, and often felt lonely and anxious. I was heading off again into the unknown, just as when our family moved from Minnesota to Illinois, only this time I was departing all by myself. On the appointed day, following another, more thorough physical, I was sworn into the military at the Chicago Induction Center. Feeling totally alone, I stood there surrounded by other recruits who looked as numb as I felt. We were then loaded onto a bus, like cattle being sent to the slaughter, and driven to O'Hare airport. There we were to board a flight to Texas where we would complete our basic training.

Having never flown caused some anxiety as we filed onto the plane and found our seats prior to the departure of the Chicago-to-Dallas portion of our journey. During the take-off, my grip on the seat's arm rests was vice-like. The fear that possessed me soon lessened and inside I felt a bit childlike and lightheaded as the plane lifted off and then passed through the low-hanging clouds. Once the jet plane leveled off, the steady roar of the engines was calming. Looking around it was clear that many of the passengers, just like me, were new recruits heading off to start a life-changing, four-year journey. Reflecting on the past and my uncertain future occupied me and probably them during most of the flight. Sitting there, I recalled my parents driving me to the Joliet train station that morning. Just before climbing aboard the train for Chicago my father shared the only piece of advice he ever gave me. He said, "Keep your ears open, your mouth shut, and don't volunteer for anything." Since he had served in the military during World War II he must have been trying to prepare me for the shock of basic training.

The second flight, from Dallas to San Antonio, was on a much older prop-driven plane. As we took off, I sat looking out a small window viewing the flames from the piston engine's red-hot exhaust illuminate the back side of the wing and a fractional arc of the pitch-dark sky. Eventually, after circling the San Antonio airfield, we dropped down to land in the dark of night. At the airport we were greeted, or barked at, by our drill instructor and then directed onto a bus and driven in complete silence through the darkness to the airbase. Since we arrived after midnight, we were lead to the mess hall, fed breakfast, and then taken to our barracks where we all collapsed into our bunks. Laying there exhausted and fearful of what lay ahead, the warm, different-smelling desert air brushed my face as it flowed through the barracks. It seemed like sleep had just arrived when all hell broke loose. To ensure we knew we were now in the military, and someone else would be calling the shots, our yelling drill instructor rudely awoke us to begin our first day of basic training at 5:00 a.m. He laid into us by loudly shouting one command after another, preceded by the word, "Airmen." "Airmen, wake-up! Airmen, get out of bed! Airmen, get your clothes on! Airmen, fall in line! Airmen, move!" Even though disoriented and fearful, I quickly threw on my clothing and fell into formation. Standing there in the dark, awaiting the command to march forward, I was sure my childhood had ended. My independence would be restricted but my optimism would not. I confidently moved forward on command to explore and experience this next phase of my life.

The Green Banana

"Let the past make you better, not bitter." Unknown

The events and situations we experience growing up can hold us back, become the focal point of an unhappy and miserable life, or motivate us to move beyond our past and strive to be different while seeking a better more fulfilling life. Throughout my childhood there were indicators that my large family's social status was at the lower end of the economic scale and that fate may have dealt me a bad hand, or as we eastside teens said, I might have been given the "green banana."

That term became part of my vernacular through my involvement in the Explorer Scouts. A major Explorer Scout activity that occurred every year was a two-week-long summer trip. The cost to participate was around $70, while the average weekly wage in the early 1960s was about $88 per week. There was never any extra money in the family budget so the idea of asking my parents for the money was quickly forgotten. A few weeks after accepting the hard facts of life, a friend talked his parents into hiring me to help paint their garage in exchange for the money required to finance the trip. They allowed me to feel good about myself, because they offered me work rather than simply money. Their generosity has never been forgotten. The trip, a grand tour of the East Coast, was the greatest experience of my life to that point. The adventure began by jamming 15 hormonally charged teenage boys, our personal stuff, and camping gear into two Volkswagen mini-buses. Our scout leader must have spent months planning and organizing this trip. Without the aid of Google maps, Trip Advisor, or the internet, he planned a full two-week excursion that included Niagara Falls, Cape Cod, Boston, Washington DC, New York City, Philadelphia, and Baltimore. He used his connections, or skillful begging, to obtain either free lodging or a place to set up our tents wherever we traveled. For instance, we spent a night sleeping with naval recruits in the Philly Ship Yard and camped on a marine base in Washington, DC. By doing this he minimized the total trip cost and limited our expenditures to purchases of food, gasoline, and entertainment.

Our road trip began with a long day of driving to Niagara Falls, which was the first natural wonder I had ever visited. Approaching the falls, the unwavering, steady roar and raw power of the rushing and falling water were like a magnet that pulled me toward the sound. I stood there in awe. While teetering on the edge of the falls, the natural wonder was captured in multiple blurred, colorless photos taken with a small, square, black Kodak camera. In a gift shop, the Niagara Falls memorabilia was bypassed to purchase a commemorative plate with the images of Jack and Jackie Kennedy for my mother. The plate hung in her apartment for decades and always reminded me of this scouting trip. When we departed in the morning we drove east toward our next stop, which was Boston. Throughout the trip whenever we entered a new state, someone would holler out the state name when he observed the "Welcome to ..." sign. With each announcement our faces peered out the window expecting to see physical changes, yet all of the states just blended together. After a brief stop in Boston to see the historical sites, we continued south to Cape Cod where we pitched our tents. Sitting near the campfire that first night I realized the difference between this campsite and all of the others was the smell of the nearby ocean. After a few days we departed and went from city to city visiting the major tourist sites like the Statue of Liberty in New York City. The ferry we boarded dropped us off on Liberty Island where a long line slowly snaked up the winding stairs that led to the viewing windows located in the statue's crown. Once the line entered the statue, we climbed the spiral staircase woven through the internal structural elements that held the statue together. It was like climbing through a jungle gym. After reaching the top, I peered out of the small, dirty windows at the view of the harbor below. It was anticlimactic, as the earlier view of the statue from the inbound ferry boat had impressed me much more. Then as the ferry boat left the dock and we headed back to Manhattan, I looked back to again get the same view my mother's parents must have had when they arrived in America. What I observed was a statue getting smaller and smaller as we moved away, while they must have viewed immense hope.

The long hours of driving in the minivans, day after day, led to some bickering and a few wrestling matches, but everyone arrived home unscarred and in one piece. It was a once in a lifetime experience for me. A term coined on that trip, getting the "green banana," is still part of my vocabulary today. It implies that an individual was given a bad deal. For instance, when we stopped in Boston we went out to eat in an old, historic seafood restaurant. An older scout who drove one of the minivans ordered a whole lobster. He planned his attack by first extracting the smaller morsels of meat from the small legs and claws before turning his full attention to the feast that resided in the tail. To his surprise, the tail was stuffed with a bread crumb mix that may or may not have contained seafood. To his credit, he raised a fuss, and was either rewarded with the proper meal or had the lobster removed from the bill. All we knew was that he had been given the "green banana."

My exposure to scouting began after being invited to join a scout troop while in grade school. Just one camping trip, which got me away from my house full of siblings, sold me on the scouts.

Since I lacked the proper personal camping gear, I used blankets rather than a sleeping bag when the weather was warm. Then there was talk of an upcoming Polar Bear campout, which would require cold weather equipment. To earn the Polar Bear badge, a scout would have to complete a winter campout between December 31 and March 1. The temperature had to be below 32 degrees Fahrenheit and we would be required to stay outdoors for at least 20 hours and sleep in a tent or shelter without any heaters for sleeping or cooking. I begged my mother to buy me a sleeping bag and we made a trip to a nearby large discount store where she made the purchase. She did not understand that sleeping bags were rated for the lowest possible temperature at which they will provide the warmth needed to stay comfortable. It would be revealed that mine was suitable for sleeping in Florida in August, for it had a vinyl plastic shell and some very sparsely distributed filling that appeared to be made out of shredded rags. After the tents were erected, my new bag was unrolled and I admired it with pride. Sometime after dark I crawled into it for the first time. It wasn't long before my shivering and shaking resembled that of a drunk who hadn't had a drink in a week. The temperature dipped to single digits on that first night – so cold that the vinyl outer shell of my sleeping bag became brittle, fractured and broke into pieces, exposing the shredded rag filling. The experience of lying there shivering in my shattered sleeping bag quickly turned my pride into embarrassment. Luckily, outside the tent, the scout leaders had started and maintained a huge campfire. A position next to the campfire, which radiated warmth, got me through the night. All night long my body rotated like it was on a rotisserie to keep all sides of me temporarily warm. After a long, sleepless night a hot meal was first on my agenda as the sun showed itself on the horizon. A cast iron skillet was heated on some hot coals and after repeatedly rapping the eggs against the side of the skillet it became clear that the eggs, along with the rest of our food, were completely frozen. Boiling the eggs turned them into something edible. As the sun continued its assent, it warmed the air and my spirits as I consumed the hard-boiled eggs. I persevered for the balance of that day and earned my Polar Bear badge. Adversity always creates lasting clear memories. That is why the events from that Polar Bear campout are as clear as a sunny winter day.

    A lack of dental care while growing up in a large family with limited resources, combined with my love of sweets, led to tooth decay and some serious toothaches as a child. My only visit to a dentist as a child was a trip to a public aid clinic. After joining the Air Force, proper dental care became available to me for the first time. A few months after arriving at my first airbase, a notification informed me to report for a dental exam. A dental assistant directed me to an examination room and the dental chair where, once seated, I said "ahhh" while the dentist quickly and loudly said, "ohhh!" I was petrified with fear and had a vice-like grip on the dental chair armrests as he looked into and probed around my mouth. Following the exam he noted dental surgery would be required to pull a few of my teeth that could not be saved. Then, following the surgery a return visit to have some cavities filled would complete my dental work. It felt good knowing dental care was in my near future but fear of the scheduled visits and what they entailed keep me on edge. A few weeks later I was hyperventilating in the dental chair as he told me to relax while he began shooting my gums full of painkiller. When he finished my whole face was numb and I was concerned, but in some way hopeful, the painkiller would spread to and numb my brain. I closed my eyes, tightly gripped the arm rests, and listened to the air suction hose that had been inserted into my mouth as he began pulling and yanking on my rotten teeth. It was a weird, unique sensation having someone pull on my teeth with that kind of force. The sound of teeth breaking under the extreme pressure of the extraction tooling, followed by a clunk in a metal collection tray, meant all was going as planned. Five of my teeth were pulled. When the dentist finished he and the nurse teamed up to carefully pry my fingers from the arm rests. They then stuffed my mouth with a large wad of gauze and sent me wobbling back to the barracks with instructions to bite down on the gauze to stem the flow of blood. My face and jaw felt like they had been worked over by a professional boxer and my gums were on gauze rags for about two days before the blood flow completely stopped and they began to heal up. A few weeks later multiple cavities were drilled and filled. Compared to the dental surgery, this process seemed easy. During this procedure I noticed how my fingers and thumbs fit precisely into the grooves located on the armrests. It was almost like the armrests had been custom made using my hands as models.

Genetics, more than my social status, were responsible for my poor eyesight. During an eye exam at my first grade school in Minnesota, I was diagnosed with less than 20/20 vision. We all believe our view of the world is honest and clear until we have a new reference point and mine was about to be re-set. Based on my school eye exam's negative results my mother scheduled an appointment with an optometrist and we made the trip into town for a follow-up eye exam. This visit confirmed the fact that corrective lenses were required and that "four-eyes" might soon be my new nickname. Then a few weeks later we made the trip back into town to pick up my first pair of glasses. The doctor's office was located on the second floor of a downtown building and we had to climb an outside wooden stairway, which angled straight up from the sidewalk to a wooden landing far above, to enter his office. After a short wait the doctor's assistant slide on and fit my new glasses. I immediately recognized a difference, but nothing prepared me for the visual experience of stepping out onto that outside staircase landing and seeing the world with corrected vision. From that elevated position, an unobstructed and clear view of the world that had not been experienced before was now visible. The bright, sunny day and my new glasses made everything viewed sharp, crystal-clear, and vividly colored for the first time. The garments hanging on a clothesline in someone's back yard resembled a brilliant rainbow. My new view of the people, cars, and storefronts on the street below led me to believe

THE GREEN BANANA

I had been transported into a new world. As my mother headed down the stairs calling out, "let's go," I lingered on the landing. I couldn't get enough of this new world. Would you just look at that! Within a year, and many more times during my childhood, my glasses broke. The money was not always immediately available to replace the broken pair. This drove some creativity involving glue and tape to make the repairs, because I liked what I saw with corrected vision.

Being the son of an alcoholic did impact my life. My father drank only beer and he drank it every day. He was generally disengaged from the parenting process, causing me to at times feel like I grew up without a father. Looking back, he could be described as a reserved, quiet man who found refuge in alcohol. He was not mean, and any anger he may have felt was pent up. There were occasional parental arguments, and in a small house they were everybody's business. Just before leaving for the military, I confronted him during one of these arguments by walking from my bedroom and shouting, "Why don't you leave her alone?" All three of us stood there a bit stunned, their argument ceased, and we all went to bed. If my father taught me anything it was the impact drinking in excess can have on both the drinker and his or her family. That left me questioning my possible pre-disposition to alcoholism and strengthened my resolve not to head down that path. Other than some experimentation with friends, drinking alcohol as a teen was avoided. Therefore the answer to the question of my dependency wasn't answered until my departure for the military.

Leaving home expedited the process of growing up. Despite the controlled environment of the military, adult decisions unrelated to military duty required answers. Joining the military at 18 provided the chance to legally kill or be killed in Vietnam, while buying and drinking a beer was illegal in Illinois for those under 21. That changed immediately upon my arrival at my first airbase following basic training. The airbase was in Louisiana, where the drinking age was 18. At that point in my life I had never been intoxicated or even seriously buzzed. My drinking education began by experimenting with different drinks at a local bar. Rather than beer, because of my father's love of it, my choices were a scotch or a glass of Drambuie on the rocks. Sipping and nursing these drinks made a single drink last most of the night. This was a strategy to both avoid overdrinking and to conserve my limited funds. My military service had just begun and my pay level was correspondingly low. My real education occurred when it was suggested that someone with a car go off base to buy some hard liquor. The intent was to begin drinking in the barracks prior to heading to a local bar on a Saturday night. Those who had contributed some cash gathered in a friend's room to wait for the delivery. He soon returned with a fifth of very cheap gin, which may have been responsible for coining the term "rotgut gin." We mixed the gin with cans of 7-Up, purchased from the barrack's vending machine, to get our buzz on. I had my first drink and then went to my room to get dressed in my finest civvies. After returning to my friend's room we continued to drink, joke around and wait for our planned departure time. During my third drink a funny sensation that caused me to feel disoriented overtook me. I stood up and slowly made my way back to my room while trying to grip the walls of the hallway. Just after opening the door to my room and collapsing onto the bed, the room started to spin. The spinning continued as my friends entered the room and shouted, "Let's go, Hafey." Their voices were loud and clear, but my body was immobilized. Though in a stupor, it was clear a poor decision had been made. My adult drinking education had begun in earnest. The first question that entered my mind after awakening about midnight was "where am I?" I eventually found my glasses, grabbed my portable, battery-operated radio, and made my way out onto the second floor fire escape landing. For a while just sitting on the metal grating feeling numb, disoriented, and homesick felt like progress. Then as the warm, humid, summer night air of Louisiana began to revive me, the portable radio was switched on and the sounds of Chicago's WLS-AM radio station filled the night. The recognizable voice of a disc jockey on WLS transported me back home to familiar places, family, and friends. By closing my eyes while listening to the popular music filling the night air, I temporarily escaped from my situation. When I reopened them, my location and now-throbbing head ensured I faced reality. Before turning in for the night, a personal vow to never again drink gin, or drink in excess, was made. This one occurrence was so influential that my life has been devoid of spinning rooms.

Just a few months after that important drinking lesson I downed the first beer I truly enjoyed. Working the afternoon shift meant my days were free for other activities, such as playing golf with friends. Luckily for us there was a very nice 18-hole golf course located on the airbase. Summers in Illinois can be hot and humid but my first summer in Louisiana gave me a new appreciation for air conditioning. Just thinking about walking out of the barrack's door would cause me to break out in a serious sweat. Consequently, golfing 18 holes in that combination of high heat and humidity resulted in serious fluid loss and clothing that was clinging to my body like a coiled python. Following a round of golf we went into the clubhouse to replenish ourselves with some fluids. My golf partners all ordered a beer; relentless peer pressure caused me to follow suit. What the bartender set on the bar in front of me was a seriously icy-cold beer in a clear glass bottle alongside a frosted mug that had just been pulled from a freezer. While slowly pouring the golden lager into the mug, chunks of beer ice crystals floated to the surface. My first drink reminded me of a slushy from a 7-Eleven convenience store. The beer slushy was so refreshing that I continued to chug it down until the mug was almost empty. It was, and may still be, the best beer I have ever consumed. Drinking isn't bad – overdrinking is.

Another indicator of my social status was the homes we resided in. My parents never owned a home. They rented the multiple homes in Minnesota and the Joliet residence was my grandfather's property. Some might also say I lived on the wrong side of the canal. Joliet's East and West sides were separated by the Chicago Sanitary and Ship Canal which ran right through the center of downtown. The East side, where I lived, was the older, less affluent part of town and it was destined to stay that way. All of the new construction, of both homes and businesses, happened on the far West side of town.

My high school was located one block west of the canal on the near West side. It was an all-boys Catholic high school and most of the students, due to the cost of tuition, were from well-off West side neighborhoods. Almost all of my close neighborhood friends went to the large, public high school on the East side of town. Because a few of my Catholic grade school friends decided to go to the Catholic high school I asked my parents for permission to do the same. Before my four years ended the cost of my tuition was too much for the family budget. The ring of the final school bell found me sadly plodding to a janitor's closet to get a broom and dustpan while all of the other students were joyously running out of the school doors. Having to work my way through high school made me feel like I didn't belong. Getting involved in extra-curricular school activities can help break down the clicks that naturally occur. My yearbook list of extra-curricular activities was very short. It read "scouting." My circle of friends at school therefore remained small and consisted of my few East side friends and some students who were also explorer scouts. If asked, my teachers would have noted I was a mediocre student who did just what was required to graduate. With parents who had other distractions there was no pressure or encouragement to study and do better. Academically I graduated in the top 50% of my class which sounds impressive. 127th out of 254! Obviously statistics can be used to deceive. Even though my high school was a college prep school, conversations with school counselors about the possibility of going to college did not occur. Or if they did, and my memory has failed me, I would have responded that I wasn't planning to attend; the word "college" was never mentioned at home. College would have involved tuition expenses, and the finances were not available. I graduated and went to work. College would have to wait until after my military service.

Because our family was so large and financial resources were so tight, we never went out to eat. It wasn't until my high school years when part-time work provided the resources that allowed me to visit restaurants. There were no restaurants in our neighborhood, other than a hot dog stand that was open seasonally, and fast food restaurants were just starting to appear in Joliet. The first local McDonald's restaurant opened in 1956 on the far West side of town. My first meal there was in the early sixties. The french fries at McDonald's were delicious while the 20-cent hamburger was forgettable. It had sat in the steam chest too long and became so dried out that trying to remove the top of the bun to add mustard was like trying to pry open an oyster with your fingertips. Dunking the sandwich in the mustard was the only option.

To get to a restaurant before we owned cars, we would walk to downtown Joliet and frequent one of the coffee shops or the International House of Pancakes. Most often we would order 10-cent cups of coffee and sit around talking while acting older than we were. Once the IHOP opened it became a favorite destination for not only cheap coffee, but cheap eats. We consumed countless stacks of buttermilk pancakes smothered with rainbow-colored boysenberry, blueberry and strawberry syrup all washed down with the "endless cup of coffee." Eventually, while in my late teens, a trip was made to an iconic Joliet restaurant that attracted people from all sides of town. All towns probably have, or had, a restaurant that everyone knows or remembers no matter what his or her age or where in the world he or she currently resides. Joliet may have had more than one, but the one that stands out for me is Merichka's. This family-owned-and-operated restaurant began in 1933 and is still open for business today. Restaurants tend to have life cycles similar to that of fruit flies, so any restaurant that lasts for over eighty years must have or provide something special or unique to its customers. Merichka's unique offering was a severe case of garlic breath! More specifically, garlic breath caused by eating one of their iconic garlic po'boy steak sandwiches. It was composed of a thinly cut, tenderized portion of beef served on a length of French bread that had been drenched in garlic butter. I quickly learned that licking my fingers in public was necessary, as each bite of the sandwich caused garlic butter to run down my fingers. To me this sandwich had just the right amount of garlic – lots! The next day the garlic started to seep from every pore on my body causing people to recognize me as someone special. Maybe that is the secret to the restaurant's longevity – the food makes people feel special.

The anticipation of feeling special at Christmas was always an empty promise that reinforced our family's economic status. Christmas morning most often found me feeling sad and disappointed. All the expectations, driven by the holiday sales and marketing hype in the stores and on television during the weeks leading up to the holiday, were dashed on Christmas morning. Under the tree might be one meager gift which may have been donated to a toy collection center prior to me receiving it. As a result, food traditions quickly took the place of gifts for me during the holidays. Each holiday season my mother made an eastern European pastry called Potica. She began by making a buttery, sweetened yeast dough that she would leave to rise. While the dough was rising, she would grind several pounds of walnuts using a manually operated cast iron grinder that she would clamp to the kitchen table. The ground walnuts would be added to a pot that contained simmering milk, sugar, and honey. The walnut filling would then be left to cool before whipped egg whites would be folded in to lighten the filling. The dough was then divided and rolled as thinly as possible into large, oval sheets on the dining room table. The walnut filling would be spread in a very thin layer on the top surface of the dough. Starting on a long edge, the dough was rolled up onto itself until you had a long, cylinder-shaped pastry. Next, the cylinder of dough was coiled snail-like into a large roasting pan and left to rise before it was baked. As it baked it perfumed our house with the smell of Christmas. That smell, and the anticipation of it, became the joy of Christmas. I no longer needed gifts and was never again disappointed.

My family's financial situation was a part of my upbringing that I couldn't control. Yet, as a child, the experiences that accentuated and affirmed our lack of financial resources strengthened my resolve to take responsibility for my adult life and make it different. If I was dealt a bad hand in life it was clearly understood the hand could be improved. Green bananas eventually ripen.

Cursing the Astronauts

Trying to find one's place or to "fit in" is a never-ending quest for all children. My first attempts were to find my place in a large family. Being second oldest in a family of nine children meant there was quite an age spread between the oldest and youngest. When I entered the military at age 18, my two youngest siblings were under 5 years of age. We were from two different generations. Even though all nine of us lived in the same house, we did not spend a lot of time together other than at family meals or in front of the television when younger. Events that might help build bonds between siblings, such as family outings, vacations, or going out to eat in restaurants never happened. With eleven people living in cramped quarters, a way out of the house always topped my to-do list. The siblings on both sides of me, in birth order, were girls. Boys don't hang out with their sisters once they have friends of their own. That made the brother closet in age to me four years younger. There was one occasion when someone had bullied this younger brother and my mother encouraged me to defend him and the family name by teaching the bully a lesson. Boy was that a mistake. After confronting him and telling him to pick on someone his own size he did – me! The confrontation resulted in the tormentor having me pinned against a porch inner wall, with my head in a head-lock, while he pummeled my face with his fist. Boy did I teach him a lesson. I expected his fist to be sore for the next week or two. So for the most part, based simply on our ages, this younger brother and my other siblings had their own circle of friends and we went our separate ways. Age more than anything else determines our group of friends when we are children. We enter school with a group of children our age and we tend to continue to hang out with, and try to fit in with, those children for the balance of our childhood.

Any cousins that I had any interaction with were cousins on my mother's side. My mother had one brother and four sisters and together they had a total of 10 children. Once again, age and proximity pre-determined that a cousin who lived next store would be a companion and friend. Upon my arrival in Joliet he not only accepted me, but introduced me to the kids in the neighborhood. Within the first week I had been punched by a neighborhood tuff who wanted to ensure the neighborhood pecking order, and my place in it, was clearly understood. I did and then settled in to listen, learn, and make friends as the opportunities arose. My cousin and I were part of the same gang of friends for the balance of our childhood and I owe him a debt of gratitude for his early acceptance and friendship. Together we and our group of East side friends learned to socialize as we explored our surroundings and participated in an array of activities.

Just because you lived near someone doesn't mean you want to, or should be, their friend. While still very young and living in Minnesota, a location that was within my free-range boundaries was a friend's house that was down the highway from ours. I remember walking along the shoulder of the highway to get to his house while cars and noisy, large trucks zoomed by, creating small, turbulent gusts of hot summer wind as they passed. When a large truck approached, my pace would slow and my eyes would close while waiting for the oncoming gust of hot air that would cause both my striped summer tee shirt and hair to flutter as it passed. I liked that feeling. When I reached my friend's house and walked up the sloping gravel driveway, he was there waiting to greet me. He excitedly showed me a new, toy nuclear submarine that he found in a box of Rice Krispies. Clever marketing people attempted to manipulate us children by inserting toys like this small, molded plastic submarine in cereal boxes and it obviously worked based on his level of excitement. Together we read the cereal box instructions that noted if we loaded the cavity in the rear of the molded sub with baking soda, it would propel itself forward when put into a container of water. Excitedly and cautiously, fearing a nuclear explosion, we slowly filled the submarine's fuel cavity with the baking soda his mother had provided. We then carefully submerged it in a barrel of rain water at the corner of their house for its maiden voyage. We both stood there intently staring at the sub while waiting for the fuel to be activated and the sub to zoom forward. Once the water and fuel mixed bubbles began to discharge from the rear of the sub and it moved forward ever so slowly. Slowly enough that we quickly lost interest in the toy. At the base of the rain barrel were some large, flat slabs of limestone. As we stood on them waiting for the sub to speed up one of the rocks tipped to one side, causing a mouse to flee from under the rock. We immediately flipped over the rock and discovered a nest of baby mice. They were very small, pink mice, about the size of a penny, which my friend quickly collected in his hand and carried down the driveway toward the highway. He then threw the vermin, one by one, onto the roadway so they would be exterminated by the traffic. Feeling very uncomfortable with both the situation and him triggered me to leave and use the highway drainage ditch as my pathway home. I chose to stay off of the highway shoulder, fearing the same fate as the mice after realizing if people thought you were a pest they might just get rid of you. While quickly walking home I vowed to behave myself and find a new friend.

You know you are fitting in when your friends give you a

nickname. Giving someone a nickname, or at least name calling ("Hey, dumb ass!"), is a childhood rite of passage for young boys that can leave one with a moniker that lasts a lifetime. My nickname was "Chick," and its origin had nothing to do with chickens. A distant relative, Charles "Chick" Hafey, had a very successful career in Major League Baseball. He won the batting title in 1931, had the first hit in the first all-star game and had a career batting average of .317. He is also one of only two baseball hall-of-fame players who wore glasses. If we were, indeed, related, I inherited his poor eyesight but none of his athletic ability. Although he retired from baseball in 1937, which was nine years before my birth, one of my friends found his name somewhere and soon after this discovery, friends began to call me Chick. The nickname lasted until entering the service, the event that separated me from the friends who used it. It is only those friends from the old neighborhood who might use "Chick" when they address me today, which causes me to respond like it has been used every day of my life.

Some of the nicknames we used for each other as kids were endearing, while others were better quickly forgotten. A few from the neighborhood were Beer Belly, Goon, J-horse, Potato, Face and Pecker. How does a child get the nickname "Beer Belly" at the age of six or seven? Grown men with that nickname had to earn it by quaffing beer for a lifetime while growing the requisite frontal bulge. If a child is a little overweight wouldn't Chubby, Chunky, Fatty or Fatso be more age-appropriate than Beer Belly? We all had old-school first names like James, John, Joseph, Jeffrey, Fredrick, Richard, Gregory, Bernard, Peter, Robert, Daniel, Samuel, and Thomas. This was the standard naming convention in our neighborhood and it was driven by our parents who relied on the names of church saints. There must have been some hope on their part that we would possess some of the traits of our namesake saint. In my case it was not some saintly bearded guy in robes who lived long ago that inspired the name that appears on my birth certificate. Instead my name was the same as my father's and his father before him – Robert Bailey Hafey.

As children we almost always entertained ourselves. If we told a parent we didn't have anything to do, he or she would simply state, "Well, go find something to do." The only way for me to get in touch with friends was by either using the dial telephone that was on a desk in our living room or to walk to someone's house and knock on the door. "Do you want to hang out?" was a common question. This meant we didn't have any plans to do anything of substance. So to pass the time there was a whole range of activities that we used to fill each day and entertain ourselves. We participated in many activities including sports and games that not only entertained us but helped us find our place socially. Each and every childhood activity with my friends helped me to define who I was. Interacting with them helped to develop my interpersonal skills, which would allow me to fit into other social circles as my life moved forward.

A painful form of entertainment that taught us to inflict and endure pain made me a social outcast. It was a game of agility that left both participants with swollen red hands. To play one of us would be on offense and one on defense. The defensive player would hold both hands out at waist height with his palms down. The offensive player would hold his hands directly below the other player's hands with his palms facing up. Then as quickly possible the offensive player would try and slap the tops of his opponent's hands. If successful, the game would continue in the same fashion. If he missed his opponent's hand, they would change places. When playing, my hands stung and turned as red as a bottle of strawberry pop. Not being a fan of a game that inflicts pain, I shied away from playing while others, with more tolerance for pain, continued to play and utter "oohh," "ouch," "oh, shit," and "dammit!"

When tired of the physical abuse, we might grab a matchbook and play the Midwest version of table-top football. One of us would hold a matchbook vertical, with one finger, on the table in front of us while the other player would touch his thumbs together while his index fingers pointed up to form goal posts. The first player would then use the index finger on his other hand to flick the matchbook toward the goal posts. If the matchbook went between the goal posts, a point was scored. Turns were taken until one of the players reached the agreed-upon winning score. Now this was a game even I could excel at. For once I had the requisite physical attributes required to shine at a sporting game. The dexterity and strength of my index finger was equal to that of my friend's.

An outside game that required a higher level of finger dexterity and strength was marbles. Buying clear plastic bags full of beautifully colored "cats-eye" marbles at the Ben Franklin five and dime provided short-lived pleasure, for eventually they would be lost in games of "keepsies" to one of the gang who had hands that were built like a super heroes. He was a strong, well-built kid who was a bit of a bully. Without provocation he would grab the back of my neck just for fun. The vice-grip-like squeeze he applied caused my knees to weaken and my voice to raise as I squirmed to release his grip. He used the same death grip to clutch a "shooter" marble in his index finger. After a circle was drawn in the dirt, all of the players would put some of their marbles in the center before turns were taken to try and shoot the marbles out of the circle. Any marble you knocked out with your shooter marble became yours. The bully, with knuckles down, would use his supernatural thumb to launch his marble from his index finger toward the intended target marble with the velocity of a bullet. Only some sort of genetic mutation could explain a thumb that generated speeds like that. When he pulled the trigger we would all look away or cover our eyes to protect them from shrapnel just in case one of the colliding marbles shattered. One by one he would shoot all the marbles from the circle as the rest of us stood around with our mouths hanging open. Literally, we lost all our marbles when we competed against him, and it was rumored that he was secretly re-supplying the Ben Franklin.

CURSING THE ASTRONAUTS

On warm summer days when we were just hanging out, we played a sporting game that required hand-eye coordination and provided the participants the opportunity to fill their pockets with pennies. It was probably my first gambling game. Contestants would line up along a crack in a sidewalk and throw pennies toward another crack six to eight feet farther down the walkway. The individual whose penny ended up the closest to the crack was the winner and got to keep all the pennies. The winners also received the secondary benefit of exercise since they had to bend over to pick up their winnings. Meanwhile the losers just stood around losing only monetary weight.

Another entertainment activity was the building of plastic model kits. You could build cars, planes, and boats. My preference was the car kits because as an early teen, driving and car ownership were already being anticipated. A trip to a downtown hobby store or one of the new discount department stores was required to pick out a new model car kit along with the glue, paint, and brushes required to create a stunning masterpiece. After the purchase, I would set up shop in our old dirty basement and start by carefully removing the contents from the box. The first step was to remove all of the small plastic parts, by bending and rotating them, from the plastic tree to which they had been attached during the molding process. The next step was a quick, ten-second scan of the assembly instructions before the gluing together of the model. This was a delicate operation that determined whether my finished model car would end up a showpiece or a piece of crap. The runny glue, if applied too generously, would run onto the surfaces that had to be painted later, thus destroying the finished look of the car. The often-warped mating pieces would not hold together if just the right amount of glue was not applied. Rubber bands, tape, string, and other assorted holding devices were used during the glue-up process in an attempt to hold the model together until the glue had hardened. Performing the glue-up assembly step required me to lean over the parts while inhaling the noxious glue. It caused lightheadedness and was probably harmful, if not toxic. Once the model was glued up and tied up it was left to sit for a day or two. The next step was to apply the brightly colored odorous paint, which came in very small glass bottles, with tiny brushes. Anyone who ever tried to paint a plastic model with a small brush quickly discovered, like me, that it was impossible to get a good finish on a plastic part using a brush. After the paint had dried, the next step was to apply the colorful highlighting decals, which came with the kit, to give the car a realistic finished look. My completed cars were a real source of pride if viewed under poor lighting conditions with squinted eyes. My optimistic view of the world always led me to believe the next car kit would be easier to assemble and the finished car would look even better.

Roller skating rinks were another entertainment option that provided a place to hang out with my friends. They were large, open, barn-like buildings with hardwood flooring. Skating was always in a dizzying circular pattern accompanied by extremely loud organ music. Once laced into my first pair of rental roller skates, ice skating never again entered my mind. Standing over and balancing on eight wheels versus two thin blades of steel was much better for my ankles, and quite a confidence builder. A low center of gravity resulting from my short stature had me quickly and confidently zooming around the rink. It was an exhilarating experience to go that fast while right on the edge of being out of control. The schedule of activities at the rink was managed by the organist who would announce the type of skate (couples only, slow dance, free skate, and reverse direction, etc.) before starting to play the next song. I never owned my own skates so my first stop after arriving was at the rental counter. The rental skates were usually well worn, or worn out, in more than one way. The shoe portion of the skates were so worn out they would flop down, like a dog on the floor, when you took them off. The insides had no padding so the metal attachments that held the wheel brackets to the sole would blister the bottoms of my feet unless two pairs of socks were worn. The skate's wheels, a critical part of a roller skate, were often severely tapered from wear. The taper was caused by everyone skating in the same circular direction and leaning into each rounded curve. The worn, tapered wheels helped me get through the curves, but when skating on the straight-a-ways they tended to pull me toward the center of the rink where, as my arms flailed to try and maintain my balance, others might have thought a pirouette was in progress. The worst-case scenario occurred when the announcer called "reverse skate." As everyone wearing rental skates skated in the opposite direction the tapered wheels on the rental skates wanted to gradually push us into the walls of the rink. We were like stars and planets that had lost the gravitational pull offered by the center of the rink and were all spinning outward into another galaxy. No doubt this was a deliberate, planned action by the owners of the rink to redirect us from the skating surface and ultimately toward their well-stocked concession stand to purchase some sugary treats. Once the skating ended we all headed outside where the quiet was deafening. The over-exuberant organist's use of the volume controls left my ears buzzing. Unbeknownst to him, he was prepping me for the rock and roll concerts in my near future.

Renting footwear reminds me of another sport that would occupy winter Sunday afternoons – bowling. Personal ownership of the required bowling equipment was out of the question, but the bowling alley would rent or provide what was needed as part of the lane rental fee. Renting a pair of ill-fitting bowling shoes was never a problem, but finding a bowling ball that could be successfully thrown down the lanes was almost impossible. All the stylish, multi-colored, misshapen rental shoes appeared to be decades old and never fit when I asked for my actual shoe size. The question "what size shoe do you wear" had no relevance to the size of the bowling shoes needed. My response was, "I wear a size seven but let me try on those fives – they will be fine." Once shod in a pair of anti-theft-colored bowling shoes, the futile hunt for a suitable bowling ball would begin. It required an almost-endless search of racks containing used and mostly useless bowling balls. Just like all Ford model-T cars, almost every bowling ball in the racks was black. The differences were the finger hole sizes, their placement and the weight of the ball. Because of my small stature, the first requirement was a ball I could lift. Bowling ball weight can vary from 6 to 16 pounds. Knowing the heaviest ball that could be lifted and launched down the lane was advantageous resulted from a discussion in math class about the relationship between mass and energy. A six-pound ball thrown by a young lad like me would probably bounce off of the pins, and a sixteen-pound ball, should my fingers get stuck in the finger holes, would dislocate my shoulder and then drag me down the lane screaming just before slamming into the pins. After a fruitless search for a ball that fit my fingers, the selection criteria were narrowed to one that could be lifted and had three holes in it. Always seeking a better-fitting ball, a return trip to the racks was made after every throw. Just as much time was spent looking over the bowling ball inventory as was spent bowling. On the plus side, we all improved our math skills while keeping score and had a fun, shared experience. We reveled in both the individual accomplishment of an occasional strike and the group ridicule and laughter that occurred when one of us tossed a gutter ball. Before leaving, I would secretly hide my black bowling ball near the end of a rack full of black bowling balls so it could easily be found the next time we bowled. Of course, it never could be.

The ultimate opportunity to entertain ourselves and hang out together came on a hot summer evening when the gang made the decision to sleep outside. A tent would be pitched in someone's backyard and everyone would haul his sleeping bag or blankets and a pillow into the tent. We staked out our piece of ground in the tent by setting up our bed and then killed time by hanging out at Heggie Park or playing cards in the tent. We waited for complete darkness, like vampires, so we could meander around the neighborhood in search of big adventures. In reality, most of our time was spent just walking in the dark while talking and laughing. If it was late enough in the growing season we might sample tomatoes or cucumbers from a local backyard garden. I almost shit my pants when we were in someone's pitch-dark garden attempting to harvest a healthy snack when the owner of the garden shouted out his back door. We scattered in different directions, and when we met up we discussed our braveness with stuttering voices and knocking knees. Stealing vegetables should be done in absolute silence, but as teenage boys, we were unable to keep quiet. More than once our noisy travels and intrusions triggered porch lights to illuminate the night, which in turn caused us to flee down the street leaving a long trail of laughs and giggles. Eventually we would tire and retire to the tent. The laughs and giggles would continue inside the tent until early in the morning when exhaustion led to sleep and finally silence. Just a few hours later, the early morning sun would rise and slowly and steadily heat the humidity-filled tent crammed with six to eight sleeping boys. When the heat became uncomfortable, I would get up and drag myself and my bedding materials home to take a nap. Unsupervised events like sleep outs gave me a real sense of independence and taught me about sleep deprivation and communal living. As it turned out these were valuable life lessons for someone who would come of age in the late-sixties hippy culture.

Halloween was an entertainment activity for both the children and adults in our neighborhood. For two consecutive nights, we had the opportunity to forage the entire East side of Joliet for candy, which provided me with sugar highs and contributed to my mouth full of dental cavities. My costume was the same every year and it required no financial investment. I was always a hobo. Getting into costume began by igniting the end of a used wine bottle cork and letting it burn until the end was charred black. Once the cork had cooled, the charcoal was rubbed on my face to replicate a five-day beard before donning an old, brimmed hat and an oversized suit jacket to complete my costume. The synchronized ignition of hundreds of corks on the eastside of

Joliet probably contributed to global warming, for countless children with five day beards were observed each night. The gang would strike out by 4:30 each day and then range near and far in search of the homes doling out the best candy. If one of us scored a full-sized candy bar we would stop back at the same house an hour later while hoping they could not distinguish one hobo from another. We never stopped until well after dark and by then the candy collection bags were so full of candy it was a struggle to carry them home. Darkness often prevented me from seeing what was being thrown into my bag, so upon my arrival home, a section of the living room carpet was staked out and the entire contents of my bag was dumped into a pile. Each piece of candy was then segregated by type and personal preference. Full-size candy bars were as rare as a double rainbow and they were certainly the Halloween grand prize. Hard candies like root beer barrels or butterscotch rounds were the least desirable simply because they took too long to eat. Sucking on a hard candy for ten minutes seemed like a waste of time when a miniature candy bar could be consumed in less than 20 seconds. One of the advantages of having so many siblings was the opportunity to trade undesirable candy for something more to my liking. Trading four or five hard candies for a miniature candy bar was like winning the lottery. Because of all the candy I consumed on that first night, my metabolism was like a hummingbird's – a bit twitchy and requiring an almost constant intake of sugary substances to keep me going. Before going to bed, I would stand in front of the bathroom mirror and look at the smudged face of an exhausted young hobo before using soap and water to make him disappear until the next Halloween. For a few weeks after Halloween, my regular school lunch, a peanut butter and jelly sandwich, was supplemented with some choice pieces from my candy collection. Then eventually the candy collection bag would run dry and I would suffer through candy withdrawal. At times, it was so bad I would beg a sibling to give me a root beer barrel.

Dressing up in a Halloween costume did not help me to "fit

in or find my place," for while in costume I escaped reality and pretended to be something I was not. Another activity, scouting, required a costume, a scouting uniform, and provided many opportunities to interact with others. Scout camping trips were a regular and very enjoyable part of my childhood. While camping, cooking meals can eat up a lot of the time available to participate in other fun activities. Cooking, and then the required clean-up at the end of each meal entailed hauled and then heating water before we could clean the dishes. In total, we could easily spend two hours of good daylight cooking, eating, and then cleaning up. One of the older scouts was aware of this time suck, so when planning the menu, he recalled a new product that had just hit the food stores – Carnation Instant Breakfast. On the first morning of the campout, when we were anticipating a large stack of pancakes smothered in sticky sweet syrup or crispy bacon and scrambled eggs, he pulled out a box of instant breakfast packets. Indignation and disbelief followed. A few of us cursed the space program and the astronauts under our breath, as they were certainly responsible for the development of this new product. After we settled down and realized this is all we had to eat, we asked the bright fella who planned the menu for the milk we were supposed to mix the powdered substance into. "Milk, I didn't buy any milk, just mix it with water," was his response. Growls and groans emanated from our mouths and stomachs until lunchtime when both were soothed with a real meal. That was the last time instant breakfast appeared on our campout menus because we all felt like we had been given the "green banana."

It felt like I was part of something unique after becoming a member of the Explorer Scout color guard that marched in front of the high school band when they marched in parades or played at football games. Each member of the color guard, wearing his explorer scout uniform, a white helmet and white spats, carried either a flag or a white wooden rifle. Because of my small stature, a good wind might have blown me over while trying to control a flag, so a wooden rifle was always on my shoulder. It was an honor to be a member of the color guard right up until after the band paraded into the football stadium when we were free to watch the football game in a get-up that repelled girls. I quickly figured out it was better to just sit with and hide amongst the band kids in their dorky band uniforms.

Since our explorer scout troop was sponsored by the Catholic high school, we were occasionally sent out to perform community service projects. The one I recall was a late-fall, Saturday morning trip to a Catholic retreat center. We were utilized as a landscaping crew responsible for cleaning up fallen tree branches and leaves from the facility grounds. It was hard work and by mid-day we anticipated that the brothers and priests, who ran the retreat center, would offer us a hearty lunch. To my dismay lunch was a hot dog. Yes, just a hot dog on a bun – no sides, no chips, and no condiments. Since this was a retreat center the assumption was made that this was some sort of spiritual lesson, for working hard for no pay and meager nourishment was akin to bondage. We grumbled as we ate our hot dogs and all felt like we had been given the "green banana," which then resulted in a productivity decline that afternoon.

Learning to fit in with others at times required me to accept some sort of risk. A few of those experiences confirmed that I was not a risk taker. A friend reinforced the fact through his actions and a happenstance that occurred on a weekend trip. He was a young man from an immigrant family who used his hard-earned money to buy a very nice new car. It was a black, 1964 Chevy Impala Super Sport with a 327-cubic-inch engine and a Hurst four-on-the-floor shifting mechanism. It was a fast car and he liked to show off by using the horsepower the car possessed. On more than one occasion when we were out joy riding he would drive to a wooded park near our home. In the dark of night, he would drive along the single-lane, winding, tree-lined roads of the park and shut off his headlights. He seemed to get a thrill from doing this, while it had an "I'm going to pee my pants" effect on me. Recently, I heard that he had lost his life in the

CURSING THE ASTRONAUTS

Vietnam War. The news included the fact that his death was not directly related to combat activity but was instead the result of a vehicle accident. That caused me to wonder if he was driving through the jungles of Vietnam with his lights off. Just before both of us entered the military he invited me to join him on a trip to Michigan. He had a romantic interest that lived there and he wanted to visit her. On Saturday evening, just after our arrival, we planned to attend a dance at a local fraternal hall. Just as we approached the dance location, almost everyone was streaming out of the entrance because an accident had just occurred on the highway a short distance from the hall. The tragic event started when a motorcyclist departed the dance and pulled onto the far lane of the highway to go left. He had plenty of time and room to clear the oncoming semi-trailer truck that was coming from his left in the near lane, but he had no idea a car was passing the truck and hidden from his view by the semi. That motorcycle accident was and still is the worst accident scene I have witnessed. Sleep eluded me that night and I accepted the fact that I was a chicken and would not, going forward, be taking risks like motorcycle ownership. My optimistic outlook stalls quickly when real risk is evident in a situation.

Learning to play poker with friends was a great way to learn about my tolerance for risk taking. Playing cards as teenagers was a summer activity that occurred during mid-week when some of our houses were devoid of parents because they were off at work. When the word spread that a game was on we would walk and jangle to the selected location with enough pennies in our pockets to almost pull our pants down. We would gather around the kitchen or dining room table, stack our pennies in a pile in front of us, and practice risk taking. Penny poker was the activity but it was dealer's choice when selecting the particular poker game to be dealt. Five-card draw and seven-card stud were standard fare. Some of the games were crazy and required more concentration than school math tests. The game of baseball was one of those card games that proved gambling, or at least playing poker, could be an educational experience. All 3's and 9's were wild and if you were dealt a 4 you received a free card. Even having what I considered a good hand would cause me to sit there and sweat, not knowing if there was any chance of winning because of all of the wild cards available. If one of us had a straight flush we were at least guaranteed to split the pot.

Other card games, for the more serious gamblers, took courage and those without it, like me, either sat out the hand or quickly dropped out. "Guts" was one of those games. Only three cards were dealt to each player by the dealer and each player then had to declare if he had guts (thought he had the winning hand) or drop out. If someone declared "guts" and then his hand of cards was topped by someone else's who had also declared "guts," the loser had to match the pot. These games could go on for some time and the ever-growing pile of pennies, if not centered on the table, could cause structural damage to the table. If someone was going to lose big and walk home with empty pockets, this was the game that would be responsible for it. Growing up with eight siblings and not a lot of money around the house caused me to feel uncomfortable with these games of more extreme chance. I always preferred the games where you were dealt a full hand of at least five cards. Since these games were longer and more involved, there was time to mentally assess my opponents and their possible hands. The self-inflicted pressure caused by the possibility of losing a pile of pennies helped to reveal our true personalities. The winners were always gloating while the losers would whine and shout, "Just deal the fucking cards!" Card playing confirmed my low tolerance for risk taking.

All the childhood activities that included interactions with others taught me how to engage with and communicate with others. I learned to trust others and the decisions I made. Saying "no" when situations made me feel uncomfortable was accepted by my friends, for trust and respect had been built during our shared experiences.

It Takes Faith to be an Angel

I was raised a Catholic, but it didn't stick. My mother introduced me to this faith when she enrolled me in Catholic grade schools. Once in school, the nuns, along with the parish priests, were the keepers of the faith who were not just charged with my education but my spiritual enlightenment. My first real Catholic memory was formed at the start of kindergarten in Mankato, MN. At the time, there were no pre-schools to help me adjust to being away from home and my mother. One day I was just dropped off at a new place with unfamiliar children and adults, causing me to burst into tears. Despite feeling like my free-range childhood was suddenly over, I made it through that first day and within a week or two going to school became a routine part of my childhood. My memories of my first school are few, apart from a hot lunch program and having to eat canned, gray, mushy peas. Of course, the nuns tried to link every aspect of life to religion. They shared numerous stories about the starving children in China and Africa before threatening us with bodily punishment if we didn't clean our plates. It seemed obvious to me that they should send the unwanted peas to China and Africa. This option wasn't presented to them because the nuns scared me. Solutions like our family dog under the table or a large napkin that would hold the gray, slimy mass were unavailable. The only answer to making them disappear – choking them down – resulted in a childhood interspersed with moments of irrational fear whenever canned peas appeared. This, my sole memory from the first Catholic grade schools I attended, did nothing to bolster my faith.

After my family moved to Joliet, I was enrolled at SS. Cyril and Methodius, the Slovak school, located about five blocks from home. The nuns who taught me there, like most nuns, were dedicated ladies who worked for next to nothing since they had taken a vow of poverty. That is why a Catholic school education, utilizing these almost cost-free teachers, was somewhat affordable during my childhood. The good sisters kept us in line through a variety of threats ("You'll burn in hell!"), physical abuse, and charm. Kneeling on your hands or on the radiator along with a rap across the knuckles with a wooden yard stick were both nun-approved methods of getting and keeping our attention. I had no idea my knuckles could swell up like that! One sister was fond of dragging mischievous students across the room by one of their ears. One class clown, who was often in trouble, had ears of differing lengths thanks to the nun's firm grip and steady pull. Instead of turning the other cheek, as noted somewhere in the Bible, he should have turned the other ear to prevent noticeable ear distortion. The doling out of punishment helped me to make the connection between pain and suffering and the Catholic faith. My religious education had begun in earnest.

There was no air conditioning in the school, so on hot, early-summer days when someone would complain about the heat we would hear, "You think you're hot? I'm wearing a black habit that soaks up the sun like a black Labrador retriever laying on a concrete stoop in August." Or something like that. We were told complaining was a sin and we should just suck it up and shut up or "offer it up." Our teachers who chose to lead a life of suffering and denial expected us, the children of optimistic parents who had suffered and been denied during the Great Depression and World War II, to do the same. Their chosen lifestyle, in a society with increased prosperity, mobility, education levels and lifestyle choices, seemed unappealing and rooted in medieval history.

Using the fear of death and eternal damnation in the fires of hell was part of the religious studies curriculum and it dovetailed nicely into social studies in the mid-sixties when the threat of a Russian nuclear attack was deemed a real possibility. I remember feeling both confused and fearful when we were instructed to get into our life-saving positions as we practiced for a nuclear attack. We were drilled to crawl under our desk and get into a sitting position with our arms under our legs and our head forward against our knees. From my perspective, the only reason to get into this position was so when my crispy, charred body was discovered, it would have looked like I was kissing my ass goodbye! Once while sitting in class, when the weather was warm and the windows were open, the roar of a large, low-flying airplane passing directly over our school caused many of us to scramble to the floor and get into the "my ass is toast" position. Our teacher calmed us down and noted the plane was making repeated passes to spread chemical pellets that would stop the spread of tree killing Dutch elm disease. As young children we were unaware of the harmful effects that would occur to the natural world around us as a result of this chemical warfare. Years later, a book titled "Silent Spring" included local accounts of the environmental damage done by the plane that flew over my classroom in Joliet. Putting one's faith in a church or science to solve the world's problems can lead to disappointment.

My grade school, like most, had a small store nearby that sold penny candy, which helped to make the long school days tolerable and strengthened my faith in humanity. During recess and lunch, drooling students would flock to the store to purchase the candy they craved with the little money they possessed. About this time I had started collecting coins using those navy blue coin collection folders that had circular openings with a year written below each opening. The talent to be a coin collector was within my reach since all that had to be done was to match the date on the coin with the correct slot in the folder and insert the coin. My collection was stored in folders for pennies, nickels, dimes and quarters. To fill the folders, my friends and I would walk to a downtown bank and trades our rolls of pennies, nickels and dimes for new rolls of the same. We would then go home and examine each and every coin to see if it was one we needed for our collection. The reason I was never able to completely fill my coin collection folders, or became a serious coin collector later in life, was that candy store next to the school. Routinely stealing coins from my collection books, to support my candy habit, caused bouts of Catholic guilt. With the pilfered money in hand, I dutifully waited in line at the candy store. The store counter with all the brightly colored candy choices on display would short circuit my brain. There were just a few moments to make my candy choices before the kids behind me and the store clerk began to pressure me. Would it be the Necco wafers, the Dots on a roll of paper, the pastel, candy-coated Licorice Snaps, a Turkish Taffy, Mary Janes, a Sugar Daddy, or a box of Boston Baked Beans or candy cigarettes? One candy I wouldn't buy or eat, even if it was free, was a jaw breaker. These hard, round candies had a diameter that almost perfectly matched the throat diameter of a six year old. This fact was confirmed when, at the age of six, one lodged in my throat. Even though I couldn't breathe and my eyes were bulging out of my head, the kids around me paid me no heed. Just before turning blue and passing out I considered a prayer, but luckily the jaw breaker was coughed up. As I gasped for air, I swore off jaw breakers – but not until finishing the one that was coughed up.

One of my favorite treats from the candy store was a small tray of salty pretzel sticks. Sneaking them into class and inserting the package into my open-front desk was easy. Then when sister was looking away, sneaking them into my mouth one at a time raised the stakes. It was a really good lesson in patience, a virtue-building exercise sister would have fully supported, for the pretzel could not be chewed. Being caught eating in class would lead to ears as floppy as a Labrador retriever's! So rather than chew the pretzel, I had to let it sit in my mouth and soften before discretely swallowed at the right moment. This cat and mouse game could occupy a whole afternoon. No wonder my grades weren't that great.

Any coins we had left after our visits to the candy store were skillfully removed from our possession by the nun's use of faith-inspired, guilt-driven extortion. A never-ending supply of collection containers, which resembled small milk cartons, provided us with the opportunity to feed the starving children in Africa, China and every other country in the world where there were children. Sister, who had the day before instructed us to bring in some change, walked down each aisle holding the container directly in front of each of us so we could clearly see the stick-figure-like starving children pictured on it. This shakedown caused me to reluctantly deposit my coins when I had them and continued to build my strong sense of Catholic guilt when I didn't. Once we all knew what extortion was, we were sent out to practice. Thinking they would teach us another valuable life skill, the good sisters sent us out into the community on a mission that helped me understand sales would not be my career choice. We were each given a punchboard and, with no knowledge of sales techniques, were instructed to go door to door in order to raise money for some worthwhile cause like the starving children in Africa or the nun's make-up purchases. For me, going door to door and asking people to gamble was a frightening experience. Knocking at each new door caused me to wish and hope no one would answer, while suppressing a strong desire to run away. With little faith that I would succeed, I was destined to fail. Rather than continuing the anxiety-inducing route through the neighborhood, I headed home and pulled coins from my coin collection folders to cover the remaining cost of the punchboard. Giving up my candy money so starving children would have something to eat should have made me feel good – but it didn't.

I knew the more well-to-do kids went home and their parents covered the cost of the punch board. Asking the poor to feed the poor seemed unfair. That night my dreams included a headline in the Joliet Herald-News which read, "Nuns who forced children into gambling activities arrested and jailed."

During one school year, we were taken on some sort of a field trip. In an attempt to further indoctrinate us and strengthen our Catholic faith, the good nuns would organize a field trip to a local theater so we could view a movie they deemed appropriate. Catholic schools at the time failed to educate students in the arts. They focused instead on the four "Rs" – reading, writing, arithmetic and religion. These mandatory, religious-themed field trips were therefore obvious recruiting trips, rather than a chance to explore the arts. I remember one field trip to Chicago, a city filled with outstanding museums and endless educational opportunities, which ended with us sitting in a dark, dank theater watching a movie about the miracle of somebody or somewhere. This religious movie, like all of them, was filled with unlimited sadness and grief, followed by some occurrence that was, decades later, considered a miracle. These were unconvincing story lines that I had trouble accepting. I didn't believe in the sudden and unexplainable appearances of people floating above bushes, on hillsides, or in caves. Rather than strengthening my faith, these movies made religion seem like just another science fiction story minus the Martians and flying saucers. My belief was that the usually sad-eyed main characters had made up the visions in their heads just like I did when I dreamt at night. When the movie finally ended, we filed out of the stinky dungeon of a theater and got back on the bus. I looked out the window at the city of Chicago and all it had to offer, and wondered why we didn't get to see or experience any of it.

Another element of my early education in religious faith was the requirement to attend mass. Each week, our teacher would lead us to the church for a weekday mass and my mother would take us to church on Sunday. My attendance was driven by obligation rather than choice. Given the choice, I would rather have been out roaming the neighborhood with my dog. He was an Irish-Setter named Sparky. This is a breed that can sometimes "play deaf," which is why Sparky would take off for the next county despite my screaming his name at the top of my lungs. In spite of his tendency to roam, I was in love with Sparky. He had a beautiful, long, red coat of fur that feathered from the back of his legs, tail, and ears. Exploring overgrown weedy areas together would allow me to spend the next few hours on my knees extracting the countless varieties of burrs that were hopelessly entangled in his long coat. The experience gave me sore knees, small punctures on my fingertips, and a slight interest in botany. He was a loyal friend and constant companion proven by the fact that more than once he joined me for, or more precisely, extracted me from, Sunday mass.

Attending mass in a cavernous, ornate church provided a nice, quiet place where I could get my thoughts together, day dream, study genetics, or just look for the pretty girls in the pews in front of me. Countless hours were spent comparing children to their parents while looking for the genetic traits like facial features, hair color, and stature, which had been passed on. The pomp, ceremony, and rigid structure of church never appealed to me. Every time a mass started I longed for it to end. The fact that the masses were celebrated in Latin by a priest who stood with his back to us added to my indifference. As I grew older, and I would like to think wiser, my interest quickly waned in an institution that insisted you follow rules defined by people who lived hundreds or thousands of years ago and even worse, refused to account for the changes in society and our collective intelligence, relative to those rules, since then. Even more confusing for me as a child was the supposed belief that one's church is the right and only church. If that were true, it made church seem like an exclusive club that discounted or diminished the value of all other religions and the millions of people who belong to them. Throughout my life I learned life lessons by being exposed to others' beliefs and actions that simply made no sense. One example was the fact that you could purchase indulgences to reduce your time in purgatory which, as explained by the nuns, was a location somewhere between heaven and hell. As a child, observing the well-to-do parishioners parade to the front of the church in their tailored suits and mink coats led me to believe they were on the fast track to heaven because they had plenty of money to buy indulgences. Where did that leave poor me – suffering in purgatory for an eternity? Those experiences pushed me in the opposite direction. I found I couldn't follow the rules of an organized religion that sanctioned looking down upon or thinking less of others. The exclusivity of the church, in a perverse way, taught me about being inclusive and valuing all others. All the experiences of my childhood, along with the people who influenced me, helped me to both understand right and wrong and develop my inner voice. My inner voice helped me understand that I would eventually be judged by how I treated people – all people. If I could get that right, then where or if I went to church wasn't that important. I am thankful I was introduced to, not forced into, a religion as a child. That fact helped me understand religious faith is a choice, and living a faith-filled life can simply be having faith in others.

Sparky understood my feelings regarding church attendance, for right in the middle of mass at some inappropriate time, like when the priest was anointing the host and the church interior was dead quiet, he would walk through the church doors that had been propped open due to the summer heat and wander up the middle aisle, tail wagging, to find me. Even before we made eye contact, a broad smile broke across my face upon hearing the clicking of his toenails against the hard floor of the church aisle. Though most of the congregation responded with smiles and a few giggles, my mother would quickly and sternly order me to take him out of church. After exiting the pew and giving Sparky a big hug we slowly and proudly walked out of the church. He found his best friend and extracted me from church early. He was, indeed, a good friend. When, some months later, it was decided we would move away from Minnesota, my parents told me the dog would not make the trip. I was heartbroken. With tears streaming down my face, I swore that someday I would own another Irish Setter. My faith was centered on the things I could control.

Each summer I was introduced to an outward display of faith by the Italian immigrant families and their descendants who lived in my Joliet neighborhood. Near the end of August, one block of the street just south of ours, along with the two intersections at both ends of that block, would be closed to traffic. The Santa Fortunata Festival, sponsored by a local Italian fraternal organization, would be set up:

The Joliet Illinois Society Santa Fortunata was established on the East side of Joliet around 1936-1937 with the purpose to relive the festivals held back in the "old country," Italy, specifically in the Province of Palermo Sicily, in the city of Baucina. Baucina is a city consisting of [fewer] than 1,000 families whose Patron Saint is Santa Fortunata. (Santa Fortunata)

This Italian festival brought the sights, sounds and smells of Coney Island, minus the ocean, into my back yard. Carnival rides were set up in both intersections and the street curbsides in between were filled with booths of carnival games and food stalls. At the intersection closest to our house, they set up the vomit-inducing tilt-a-whirl ride. This ride helped me to confirm my predisposition to motion sickness. Those who witnessed my first ride used phrases like, "screaming like a girl to get off," and "stumbling around while puking," to describe my actions. Ever since, my avoidance of carnival rides has been akin to a cat's avoidance of bathwater. In addition to the carnival rides, the carnies would set up and later man the carnival game booths. You could test your skills trying to knock over three leaden milk bottles stacked in a triangular shape or stuffed, cat-like figures, with fur around their perimeter, off of a shelf with baseballs. Possessing little or no money to play these games meant watching as the carnies lured in players by either telling them how easy the game was or by challenging their ego. "Come on, handsome, show your girlfriend what a great arm you've got!" It became clear very quickly that these games seemed to be stacked in favor of the carnival. Unless the three milk bottles were hit in an exact area the size of a pea you would never knock all three over. As for those fuzzy cats, they were 70% fur and 30% cat which meant most throws went between the cats. Since you had to knock three cats down to win, a winner was as rare as an honest carnie. Yogi Berra was right when he said, "You can learn a lot just by watching." After watching these games of chance, my hands and my money stayed in my pockets, for I had no faith in the possibility of winning.

My strongest memories of the Santa Fortunata Festival are three food memories. It may be hard to believe at this point in time, when you can purchase pizza by walking five minutes from wherever you are on this earth, but in the late fifties I had not yet eaten pizza. One of the food stalls sold pizza – real Italian pizza. The booth contained a large, black pizza oven that spewed searing heat and the smell of crust starting to caramelize to the point of turning black. When any of the three long, narrow doors were opened to insert or remove a pizza, the combined aromas of baking bread, bubbling and browning cheese, and oregano-spiced tomato sauce was other worldly – as in a small village in Sicily.

My second memory involves a stall that sold Italian sweets. My genetic addiction to sweets caused me to spend an inordinate amount of time around this food stall. They made pastries I had never seen or heard of, like a cannoli – a deep-fried, crispy pastry sleeve scented with the flavor of Marsala wine and filled with a sweetened, creamy, ricotta cheese filling. To gild the lily, the ends of the cannoli were dipped into shaved chocolate and green pistachios and then the whole thing was dusted with powdered sugar. This wasn't a game of chance; this was an opportunity for a taste of Italy. One year, after working at one of the food stands, I spent part of my earnings on a cannoli. It tasted even better than it looked.

IT TAKES FAITH TO BE AN ANGEL

My third and most vivid food memory from the festival is triggered by the smell that emanated from the Italian sausage stand. This food stand was massive in proportion to all the others and it took up a large area in front of the Santa Fortunata Hall. Located within its boundaries were multiple long, metal grilling trays resting on metal legs. In each tray was glowing hot charcoal that spewed whiffs of sausage-scented smoke as the Italian sausages, strung above on long metal skewers that spanned the width of the tray, dripped their juices. As the skewers of sausages perfumed the air, the Italian men would continually move them down the length of the tray. New skewers of pink sausages made from ground pork seasoned with salt, pepper, and sweet fennel seed were added at one end and the cooked, golden-brown sausages removed at the other end where the sandwiches were assembled and served. On another cooking stand were large, deep, steel trays filled with three types of peppers – sweet bells peppers, sweet banana peppers, and wickedly hot banana peppers – all of which were bubbling away in olive oil and water until they were just soft enough to melt in your mouth. Without looking you could locate the bushel baskets of locally grown and just-picked red, yellow, and green peppers by their smell alone. They sat on the ground waiting to be washed, cut up, and cooked. The combined aroma of the sausages and peppers was marketing genius. If any vegetarians attended the festival I can guarantee the alluring aroma and the sight of a crusty piece of Italian bread – filled with a grilled sausage smothered with soft, cooked peppers – challenged their faith in vegetarianism.

On the last day of the festival, a Sunday, a Sicilian band dressed in ornate uniforms would lead a religious procession from the festival site to the Italian Catholic Church in Joliet. Later in the afternoon the same band performed on a temporary bandstand preceding the highlight of the festival – the flying of the angels. Earlier in the week, before the festival began, two scaffold towers had been erected on opposing corners of the intersection closest to the society hall. Two large wooden pulleys were mounted on the top of each tower and then a large-diameter, natural-fiber hemp rope was used to connect each of the two pulley sets like enormous clothes lines. At the appointed time the band began to play and from the fraternal society hall emerged proud, faith-filled Italian men carrying an ornate glass casket that contained a statue replica of Santa Fortunata lying in repose. The extravagant religious symbol was placed on a platform that had been built on the back of a pick-up truck. Meanwhile, the angels, two young Italian girls dressed in colorful gowns and made up like they were going to the senior prom, were each taken up one of the scaffold towers and readied for their imminent flight. Before today's obligatory parental release forms and lawsuit mania the two girls, wearing leather body harnesses, were each strung up onto one of the ropes using the harness along with colorful ribbons that secured one wrist and one ankle. As the truck pulled under the center of the intersection, the ropes were pulled by the Italian men manning the platforms and then as the pulleys rotated the faith filled angels were propelled on their herky-jerky concave and bouncy arc of flight. The two angels would "fly" until they were centered over the lavish glass casket and then in unison begin a lengthy prayer by twice reciting, "Viva, Viva, Santa Fortunata!" When finished with their prayer recital, they would fill the air with colorful fluttering confetti released from one of their gown's sleeves. Then, as the pulleys were reversed, the angels flew backwards like dragonflies, although not as quickly or gracefully, while doves located in a crate on the truck bed were set free to distract the onlookers. More than once a teary-eyed angel balked at being strung onto the pulley rope, or actually cried and rained either tears of fear or intense faith onto the casket as she recited her prayers. While looking around at all the people staring intently up at the two dangling, bouncing angels, it occurred to me that it takes faith to be an angel. To me they were courageous and beautiful. After they were safely and securely back on their scaffold platforms, the truck carrying the statue drove necessarily, painstakingly slowly down the street while faithful onlookers approached the ornate glass casket and pinned paper money in long ribbons, which fluttered in the air like the freed doves, as the procession moved forward. Watching the procession caused me to wonder what they hoped their offerings of money would get them. Were they buying indulgences or a new furnace for the fraternal hall?

Just like that, the Santa Fortunata festival was over for another year, although the smell of the sausage stand lingered in the air for a few days. The following week, back in school for a new school year, I would daydream of the sights, sounds, and smells of my backyard summer festival until my Catholic grade school teacher, Sister Black Robes, tugged on my ear. This religious-themed festival truly was the highlight of my summer and ever since those special summer days, whenever Italian sausage is on my grill, this phrase is repeated twice. "Viva, Viva, Santa Fortunata!" If someone nearby asks, "What did you say?" I simply smile and say "nothing." I was communing with flying angels and they would not have understood.

Some years later, while serving in the US Air Force in the Philippines, another public display of faith puzzled and confused me. The Philippines was a third-world country. Leaving the base via the main gate to the town of Angeles City challenged my faith in humanity. This was a surrealist landscape with two different socio-economic worlds separated by only a fence and gate. My understanding of what growing up poor meant was reframed and redefined upon witnessing the filthy, deprived conditions in which the people of Angeles City lived. The first sense that was stimulated when the main gate came into view was my sense of smell. The air was filled with a putrid smell that emanated from the open sewers that lined all of the streets on the other side. Money changers and hucksters of all shapes and sizes confronted me the moment I stepped into the third-world environment. Small children would pretend to drop a quarter into my pants pocket while asking if I had change. Believing them, which is what they hoped, meant handing them a quarter. "Hey Joe, my quarter fell in your pocket," would echo behind me as I quickly walked away. Then recalling my childhood and the excitement felt when my dad or an uncle handed me a nickel or dime, I would occasionally stop and just toss one of the street rascals a quarter. My act of kindness to one only triggered the others to pursue me with a new level of intensity, causing me to increase my pace and disappear into the crowd.

Around Easter, just a few days before Good Friday, someone mentioned a kind of passion play or parade that would occur in town on Good Friday. Having been told I should not miss this display of faith inspired me to head to town on Friday morning with my new Pentax SLR camera to capture the event on film. It was hot and humid and there was a buzz in the air. People were three-to-four deep on both sides of the dusty main road leading through town. My walk continued until an open spot was found from which the roadway was visible. About 30 minutes later a noisy commotion could be heard moving down the road just ahead of the procession. Then suddenly, into my view came young men with bare upper torsos, whipping themselves as they slowly processed down the street. Their arms went back and forth, left and right, over and over as they rhythmically swung a whipping device with multiple cords. Attached to the end of each cord was a hard object that would flail their backs. With each swinging motion of their arms I could hear the flogging tools slapping their backs. Once they passed my location, their backs, red with dripping blood, came into view. I grimaced while viewing the bloody scene through the camera's view finder and continued shooting one photo after another. The first group was closely followed by second group of penitents who struggled to carry large, heavy, wooden crosses in the tropical heat. These surreal scenes viewed through the camera's lens seemed both abstract and magnetic. For the next five to ten minutes, as the procession slowly passed, I watched in utter disbelief. Puzzled by what I was witnessing, I wondered what on earth would cause people to do this to themselves. Then the act of simply lowering the camera and looking around at the squalor these poor people lived in, allowed me to rationalize their behavior. Religion attracts people in need of or lacking something and almost every Filipino was over-qualified – they needed so much. Their religious procession opened my eyes to the extremes people will go to when they are blinded by what they think religious faith can accomplish. This real-life, in-my-face religious cultural experience touched me, for I immediately started carrying more quarters in my pockets when going to town.

Watching this bloody expression of religious faith on the streets of Angeles City caused me to question why I didn't turn to religion. A childhood defined by growing up in a very large family with limited resources and a father who drank daily might push someone in that direction. But for me, those childhood experiences turned me into a realist and made religious faith seen like a form of wishing and hoping. Wishing and hoping we had more money, a larger home, and a father who spent his evenings at home rather than the corner tavern wouldn't have changed anything. Religious faith doesn't solve problems – it provides hope. It is only when someone takes action that anything changes. My free-range, exploratory, independent childhood taught me to be hopefully optimistic that most situations will turn out okay if I personally get involved in the solution. It is hard to explain – it is simply an inner feeling of confidence, both in me and those around me. It is not faith in a religious sense, but it is faith in humanity.

A Handful of Worm Poop

It didn't take long for me, a child growing up with meager financial resources, to make the connection between work, money, and my desire for the things boys want. A collection of experiences that tested my resolve, like marching 50 miles in a day, along with a series of childhood jobs, prepared me for my first real 40-hour-a-week, adult job. That occurred when I was hired to work at the US Steel plant, which was located just one block from my house, right after my high school graduation. This was a massive facility that covered many acres of property. It was adjacent to the property where the early Joliet Iron Works plant, which attracted and employed thousands of Eastern European immigrants, had stood. Not long after moving to Joliet as a ten-year-old, the mill celebrated a milestone – its fiftieth year of operation. As part of the planned festivities, management opened the mill for public tours. They had laid out a path through the facility that took the visitors, including me, through the different mills and support service buildings. The tour began with a visit to the hot mills, where 4-by-4-inch by 40-foot-long steel billets were heated in furnaces until red hot. The mill building was massive, old, dirty, dark, smelly, and hot. We watched in awe as the red-hot billets were pushed from the furnace and into roll stands where they were pulled, by rotating rolls, through a series of ever smaller rolls, in order to produce round, coiled steel rod of different diameters. As the hot steel progressed through the rolling mill, it picked up speed and length as it grew smaller in diameter. The leading end of the hot steel rod was shooting through space like a bullet just before it was coiled into a red-hot bundle of steel. This was amazing stuff to see as a pre-teen boy – it was better than television. After we departed the hot mill we walked a long way before entering the wire mill. Here the rod that had been rolled in the hot mill was reduced in diameter again to make steel wire. This was accomplished by pulling the rod through a series of ever smaller dies until it reached the expected finished diameter. Then the wire was turned into products the tour group could recognize. First we were shown a variety of fence making machines. Coils of wire were fed into these complex, clattering machines, which wove the wire into different types of wire fencing that one might use to enclose a garden or contain livestock. We also observed barbed wire being produced. The Joliet US Steel plant's barbed wire machines were old. I not only observed them on the tour but later, when I worked in this same plant, I operated these machines – some of which were originally built in the late 19th century. At least half of the barbed wire produced at this time was shipped to Vietnam. There it was used to keep the enemy out of areas rather than contain animals. Once employed at US Steel, each time a spool of barbed wire was removed from a machine, I attached a paper label that had a red, white, and blue shield on the front. Pictured in front of the shield were two hands embraced in a handshake of friendship. The people who removed this label, before uncoiling the reels of barbed wire around the perimeters of their military positions, were the soldiers from both the US and South Vietnam military. Attaching the labels caused me to wonder if they smirked at the sight of the friendly handshake label as they endured the living hell of war.

A HANDFUL OF WORM POOP

As our 50th-anniversary tour continued, the next stop was the nail department. We entered a massive room where at least 100 nail makers banged out nails at an amazing rate. Stunned by the noise level, my hands were raised to cover my ears. The machines were laid out in linear rows with aisles in between that were covered with thick steel plates. There was so much noise and vibration from the nail making process it reminded me of the electric football game friends and I played. The game consisted of a field, a thin, sheet metal surface that had been color printed to look like a stripped gridiron, held in a plastic frame. Each player would position his team, small, pressed board figures standing in small, plastic holders, on the field near his goal line. Then the game was plugged into an electrical outlet and the switch was turned on. The metal board would vibrate loudly and the players would move in erratic zigzag patterns. It was more a game of chance rather than skill for if your ball carrier made it into the opposition's end zone you scored. Standing on the steel aisle plates caused my whole body to vibrate, leading me to believe I could continue the tour without moving my feet! I didn't know it then but my first supervisory position at U.S. Steel would be in the Nail Room.

My first job at US Steel was titled "oiler." The permanent oiler was on an extended vacation lasting a full 13 weeks, giving me an opportunity to cover the job in his absence. The job responsibilities were walking around with a grease gun or oil can and lubricating bearings and other lubrication points on a wide variety of equipment. The brief job training involved a supervisor showing me around the equipment and then leaving me to work on my own. For the first few weeks my routine was wandering around hoping to be doing what was expected. My work station or, more truthfully, the place to hide when not walking around lubricating equipment, was a tunnel under the nail mill. I shared the space with the "belt man." Job descriptions back then were very straight forward. Some of the older nail-making machines were still powered by leather belts that transmitted the power from long line shafts with pulleys, which ran through the tunnels under the nail mill, to pulleys on the machine's main drive shafts. This line shaft technology was used to power equipment when water wheels turned line shafts in the 19th century. Working here was more than a job, it was a history lesson! The belt man would maintain and repair those leather belts along with rubber conveyor belts used to transport nails. When the oiler returned from his long vacation, I was trained to run barbed wire machines and then soon after went off to serve my country. After my discharge, a machinist apprenticeship and eventually a management position defined my career path at US Steel.

The term *work ethic* was first used in the early fifties. Therefore, when my mother assigned me and my older sister the job of washing and drying the dinner dishes, either she was on a moral mission or was just tired of doing the dishes herself. This chore was a tortuous event each and every evening and it was not a shared experience that brought us closer together. It was instead a daily squabble fest. As we argued about who would wash or dry, my friends could be heard playing outside and that turned my bad attitude into defiance. An allowance, which some parents might offer to take the sting out of doing household chores, was not part of this deal. With eight siblings and a shortage of cash, the word *allowance* was not part of my childhood vocabulary. I quickly understood that having spending money in my pockets meant working for it.

My first experience with getting paid for something was for a product I had helped to harvest. Close by my first home in Minnesota, the location where my earliest memories were formed, was a long sloping valley with tapered sides that was called the sheep pasture. The sheep, known for their ability to gnaw the grasses of a pastureland down to nubs, were long gone. The pasture was now overgrown and home to tangled masses of wild red raspberry vines that attracted me and my friends. Their thorny canes would tear us to shreds if we tried to walk directly through them, but yielded quarts of the finest and sweetest red raspberries if we slowly and patiently picked the ripest ones. After eating our fill, we would carefully harvest them into wooden fruit baskets before heading throughout the neighborhood, with red, stained, sticky hands, in what was my first attempt at door-to-door sales. There was some comfort being with others as we knocked on strangers' doors. As our berries were exchanged for shiny nickels and dimes, my fear lessened and I felt excited.

As children we lacked the capital investment to make some serious money so we relied on nature to provide some cash flow. Together we labored to harvest and sell a natural resource that was located right in our backyards. To start a worm business, you only had to cover one fixed expense, a flashlight. The variable expenses were the batteries. When it gets dark, night crawlers pull themselves out of the ground and seek companionship – if you know what I mean. Warm, damp nights would find us hunched over or on our knees, with flashlights in hand, looking for copulating worms. Once the end of a night crawler was grabbed – and they were slippery, little, wiggling creatures – it had to be slowly extracted from its hole with a steady pull. Pulling too hard meant the worm would break in half, leaving us holding half of a night crawler and a handful of worm poop. Finding two of them in love's embrace meant the chance to grab them both and pull the two lovers out of their respective residences at once. There were more misses than catches, for they were quick to retract themselves back into their burrows when the light and my hand movement spooked them. After a few hours of tugging and pulling, my old coffee can would be partially full of wiggling worms; while my hands were just plain disgusting. The next day my catch would be taken to the worm middle-man to make my sale. He was a barber located on the next block. His offered price for good (not broken in half) worms was 10 cents per dozen. That seemed like a get rich quick scheme, easy big money, yet it never materialized. As soon as he looked at the can of worms he would quickly scan only the top and say, "Most of them are broken and dead. Here is a quarter. You are lucky to get that." I think he was taking advantage of me, for he resold the worms for 25 cents per dozen and made a handsome profit. His penny-pinching, child-exploitation behavior caused me to question his integrity. I decided to go to someone else for my haircuts because I didn't like him and he probably had worm poop under his finger nails.

Having my hands covered in dirt and poop opened the door for me to try my hand at seasonal work on a truck or garden farm. I cannot remember who told us about this money-making opportunity, since the experience was purged from my memory the day after it occurred. I was instructed to meet at a neighborhood intersection at 7:00 a.m. at which time a large flatbed truck, with fence railings, pulled up and stopped on the white, crushed gravel roadside sending a cloud of dust billowing into the air. Emerging from the cloud were optimistic child laborers who joined me as we climbed aboard and were driven to a vegetable farm on the outskirts of Joliet. Upon our arrival, we were quickly training in the art of pulling miniscule weeds from row after row of newly planted vegetables. Spending the entire day bent over under a blazing summer sun, picking tiny weeds from rows of newly planted vegetables for 25 cents an hour was a life lesson. At the end of the day when handed my wages, $1.75 in cash money, I felt dispirited, exploited, exhausted, and underpaid. The experience caused me to wonder if my grandfather, who worked in a coal mine after he immigrated to this country, felt the same way. It only took one day of this back-breaking work for me to avoid that corner in our neighborhood, even in the middle of winter, for fear that the flatbed truck might pull up.

Cutting the neighbor's grass was another money making opportunity that my cousin and I tried our hand at. My backyard was tiny and had a fine collection of weeds, but very little grass, so it provided little experience in yard maintenance. My cousin, who lived next door, had a yard that was about the same. At one time, both of our yards may have had a lawn, for in a shed next to my cousin's house we found an old lawn mower that must have belonged to our grandfather. It was a manual rotary mower that was as rusty as the bodies on most automobiles after they were seven or eight years old in the 1950s. We tested it out in our weed-choked yards. Using this mower with dull blades required us to run toward the intended cut location at full speed. When the rotating blades engaged the grass, or in our case sparse weeds, my forward momentum would quickly slow until both the blades and I would come to a sudden stop. I would then back up and take another run at it. As my grass-cutting skills and confidence grew, the neighborhood was searched for any yards that looked like they needed a cut. After some door knocking, someone with a real lawn hired me. I soon discovered that a thick, grassy lawn has a density greater than that of our weedy yards. Upon my initial charge the blades instantly stalled, while my forward momentum almost flipped me over the mower's push handle like a gymnast flipping himself over a pummel horse. Sheer determination drove me to attack that same swath of grass over and over. No real progress was made. With my head hanging low and the mower in tow, I walked away from this money-making opportunity.

There was also wintertime seasonal work, like Christmas caroling, available for me and my cousins. Without any practice, or knowledge of all the words to the Christmas carols, we would strike out on Christmas Eve to spread some holiday cheer. We targeted houses that were well lit with Christmas decorations and echoed the sounds of people having fun inside. These were indicators that some drinking might be occurring inside and the residents and their guests might be willing to let go of some cash following our singing performance. We would approach their door, knock, and then as soon as the door opened, block the doorway with a few strategically placed feet or smaller choir members before beginning to sing loudly in differing keys and using our own made up words when we didn't know the real ones. We would continue with our unique renditions of popular carols until they rewarded us for our efforts with a cash settlement. The payment was occasionally because they sincerely enjoyed the musical experience, but most often just so they could close their doors and prevent both heat and hearing loss.

My first real job, one where I was contracted to do something daily in exchange for regular pay, was a paper route. It was an entry-level job for many young boys and girls. My route was contained within a four-square-block section of my neighborhood. My responsibility was to deliver the daily tabloid, undamaged and on time, to anyone within my route area who had a subscription. Then every two weeks I had to knock on the subscribers' doors to collect their payments, which I then delivered to the newspaper office on the following Saturday morning. Each day a truck would rumble past our house while an arm with a gloved hand would extend from the open back of the truck gripping a bundle of papers that was tightly bound with cross wires. The arm would swing inward and then outward to toss the bundle, which would thump the ground and tumble to a stop in a cloud of gravel dust alongside our house. Using old, dull pliers I slowly gnawed at the wires until they snapped. Then gripping each paper with both hands, it would be folded into thirds by tucking one of the long ends into the opening on the opposite side. This was to keep the paper from blowing away after it was tossed onto the customer's stairs or porch. Once folded, the papers were inserted into my paper bag, a canvas pouch that was slung over one shoulder. My route had 30-40 customers so the bag, when fully loaded, was a strain to carry for someone of my stature. I walked the same route, day after day, tossing papers onto, or at least at, the appropriate locations as I went. The paper toss could be quite artistic and was once considered for inclusion as an Olympic sport. The job was beneficial for many different reasons. It was physical and required mental dexterity to remember the route, the new customers, and those who had dropped their subscription. Dealing directly with people and managing both the financial records and the cash I collected when customers made their payments were all great learning experiences. Every two weeks, after multiple trips to collect from a few slackers who wouldn't answer their doors, my collection money was totaled. The following Saturday morning I would walk downtown to the Joliet Herald-News office to make my payment and collect my commission on sales. Walking out of the newspaper office with folding money in my pocket was a grand feeling. I often headed straight to Jet's Burgers to live it up a little. Jet's was a knock-off of a White Castle restaurant. For a buck and some change, I could eat my fill of those little square burgers smothered in onions and sandwiched between warm steamed grease soaked buns. Both the burgers and the job were satisfying. For the first time, I felt like I was part of something, contributing to society, and being fairly compensated for my efforts. I didn't just have a paper route; I was part of a news organization that kept people informed and I was putting money in my pocket.

During my high school years, one of my summer jobs was at a fruit stand. It was owned by a sometimes cantankerous, but most often kind, old Greek gentleman. The fruit stand was located on a corner in a low, flat-roofed building with four garage type doors, that when opened, allowed passing customers to see directly into the storefront. Within the building were a variety of makeshift wooden tables on which the produce was displayed for sale. Unlike today's sterile grocery store produce departments, none of these tables were refrigerated. The produce, after being removed from a walk-in cooler, was taken from the shipping cartons and neatly stacked on the tables. If the produce sold quickly everyone was happy – especially the owner. The problem with this "no refrigeration" business model is that when items did not sell quickly enough they would begin to decay and rot. This caused a few problems. The first being flies who had a free-access pass to the inventory because the storefront was wide open. The fruit flies were so numerous that if they grouped together and flew in front of the sun, some customers thought a solar eclipse had occurred. We didn't bother trying to control fruit flies. Their life span was measured in hours and they were individually almost impossible for us or our customer to see, so instead we battled the larger and more annoying common house fly. We all became very skilled at using a fly swatter. So skilled, in fact, that it became boring, so when the owner was away we started using our bare hands in a competitive game requiring cunning, dexterity, and speed. When a fly would land on a surface I would cup my hand and as quickly as possible swing my arm in an arc so that the cupped hand would intercept the fly just as it was taking off. At the moment of contact my hand would close to try and capture the little disgusting insect that was capable of laying 8,000 eggs that would hatch into 8,000 wiggling maggots. A quick shake of my hand would let me know if my attempt had been successful. The next step was to throw the fly against a flat table surface as hard as possible. If done correctly the fly would hit the flat table and bounce into the air only to fall back down dead. If done incorrectly, primarily due to a lack of arm speed and therefore fly velocity, the fly would bounce lightly and then fly off. Successful kills were scored and the clerk with the most kills would win! This is one of those life skills I have not been able to apply elsewhere.

The second problem with rotting fruit and vegetables was that we had to constantly sort through the inventory to remove the bad stuff. Nothing turned off a customer more than grabbing a rotten tomato or peach. This was a pet peeve of the owner, so he was constantly inspecting his inventory to ensure we had removed anything unsavory. To replenish the store's inventory the owner used a large truck to make re-supply trips to either the wholesale produce market in Chicago or to Michigan to pick up freshly picked fruits when they were in season. For him, peach season was a big deal and an opportunity to make a killing. Customers would anticipate the season so when the peaches arrived they would buy them, by the bushel or half-bushel, to make jam or can them for use during the winter. So twice a week during the peak of peach season the owner would select someone to drive the truck and off they would go to Michigan to buy Red Haven peaches. The downside of purchasing a truckload of peaches, when they were just picked and almost at their peak of ripeness in the heat of late summer, is their shelf life is measured in hours rather than days. If they didn't sell quickly, any peach with a little bruise acquired during the picking or transport processes quickly became a softening, brown spot that began to grow a gray, fuzzy coat of mold. Sorting through bushel after bushel of peaches to remove the fuzzy ones became a full-time job.

One day I woke up feeling sick. The owner had given me the job title "manager" and paid me $10 a week more than my peers. This meant opening the business when the owner, who earlier that morning had left for Michigan to buy a truckload of peaches, was unavailable. Due to my illness, no attempt was made to search for the fuzzy peaches in the existing inventory. When the owner returned, the newly purchased peaches were unloaded and then he began to inspect the old inventory. As he found fuzzy peaches he began to throw them on the floor. *Splat, splat, splat* was the sound made by the rotten peaches as they exploded on the floor. It was his way of letting me know I hadn't done my job and the mess was mine to clean up. Informing him that I woke up sick and forced myself to come into work so the store would be open didn't impress him. He replied that he didn't care. I removed my blue and white striped apron, threw it at him, and quit. About 30 minutes after arriving home, the fruit stand truck pulled up to my house and one of my co-workers said, "The boss wants you to come back to work." I quickly and confidently hopped into the truck's passenger seat knowing I had just stood up for myself and won.

The aprons we wore were also a source of fun when business was slow. More than once someone stapled the apron strings together at the back of a co-worker's apron. If done without them sensing it, which was a tricky and difficult task, plenty of laughing occurred later when they attempted to untie and remove their apron. Once when an attempt was being made the apron wearer reached back to stop the culprit only to have the palm of his hand stapled to the apron string. The staple had not only entered the soft part of his lower palm but had been fully curled and set. Our laughs hastily turned to words of advice like, "just pull it out – it will only hurt a little," or, "let's use the razor knife used to open boxes to pry open the staple or cut your skin." We quickly lost all interest in this prank.

My next job was at a fast food restaurant on the south side of Joliet that served flame-broiled hamburgers. It was similar to the newly opened McDonald's and Burger King restaurants that had been constructed on the more affluent west side of town. The owner was an independent businessman and the restaurant bore his name. My duties were centered on assembling the hamburgers. Beef patties were positioned onto a rotating wire conveyor that moved them through a stainless steel rectangular tube containing open flame gas burners that would broil the patties from both the top and bottom. At the discharge end, the cooked patties would slide from the conveyor and down a chute where they would be retrieved and placed on the buns with the appropriate condiments. For my lunch I would broil four patties and stack them on a slice of bread with cheese, ketchup, and mustard in between each patty. It was topped with the second piece of bread before being consumed as hot grease, ketchup, and mustard ran down my hands. Today it doesn't sound that healthy, but it was really good and the word cholesterol was not part of our vocabulary yet!

This place of employment was also the location of my first automobile accident. One day a car-less friend, whose girlfriend lived on the near west side of town, asked for a ride to pick her up. The return trip was on a route that passed by my place of employment, so we decided to stop for something to eat. A parking spot right up front next to the building was open. Coasting toward it my foot reached for the brake petal. When I depressed it, it went right to the floor and the car, almost as if it was in slow motion, bounced slowly up over the curb. This part of the building was really a glass-enclosed extension that would keep the customers dry and warm in inclement weather. As the car slowly bounced up and over the curb, it just barely touched the metal frame containing a large pane of glass. As the glass loudly shattered into a thousand pieces the customers who were inside screamed and ran in the opposite direction. I was short and attempted to make myself shorter by shrinking in my seat as everyone stared at me. This was one of the most embarrassing moments of my life. Driving your car into the building where you work seems like a story someone would have to make up, but it really happened. The owner of the business reacted like the gentleman he was. The mess was cleaned up, the insurance claim was filed and the occurrence was forgotten by all except me and a few friends who will never, ever, let me forget it.

Other childhood experiences also helped prepare me for a lifetime of work. Starting and completing long hikes while in the scouts strengthened both my resolve and my physical endurance, while providing a real sense of accomplishment. There were three 20-plus mile hikes in northern Illinois and I hiked all three. The first was the Blackhawk trail in northern Illinois. It was named after an Indian chief, a prominent historical figure in the early 1800s, who was born in a village along the Rock River. The second trail was near Starved Rock and Buffalo Rock state parks in north central Illinois. Most of this trail followed a two-lane blacktop road, which meant we walked on pavement, or the gravel shoulder of the road, which resulted in tired aching feet. The third hike followed a towpath along the Illinois and Michigan Canal, a scenic and historical route. The building of this canal, used to transport bulk goods like the limestone mined in the Joliet area, in the mid-eighteenth century brought many Irish immigrants to the Joliet area. This trail followed the well-worn path used by the mules that pulled the barges along the canal route. For any outdoor activity like hiking, having the right equipment is important. Today there are so many different types of sport-related shoes a guy's closet could easily be mistaken for a girl's. On my long, grueling scouting hikes I wore my one pair of shoes. They were the same shoes worn everywhere for I only possessed one pair at a time. The early excitement of starting out on any new trail waned quickly and before we reached the trail's end, whether one was wearing hiking boots or street shoes, we were spent and whining. These endurance hikes built character and helped to prepare me for the big one – the Kennedy March.

I had a personal connection to President Kennedy, as I once touched his hand. This occurred during an election rally when he visited Joliet on October 25, 1960. As a planned motorcade made its way down Chicago Street, my friends and I had secured front-row positions on the curb. From here we had a clear view of the future president as he sat on the trunk of a convertible with his feet resting on the back seat. As his car approached our position, some people rushed toward his car to try and shake his hand and we quickly followed suit. I didn't get a hand shake, but I did get a touch. It was my first brush with someone famous and that made me feel excited and special. Caught up in the excitement, we next made our way to a downtown hotel where Kennedy would dine that evening. As we stood in the lobby crowded with reporters and supporters, we caught another glimpse of a man who possessed a sort of magnetism. Then just over three years later, while walking into my high-school cafeteria, the news that the president had been shot was being talked about by everyone. During my afternoon classes I remember feeling stunned and unable to focus. After arriving home and switching on the television I sadly watched, with the rest of the nation, as the shocking events of the day were unfolded before us. To me he seemed to be an inspirational leader – probably because of his youthfulness. Between the time when our hands touched and his death he inspired me to do something challenging – to walk 50 miles in one go:

John F. Kennedy came into the Presidential office with a goal of improving the health of the nation as part of his New Frontier. As President-elect, he wrote and had published an article in *Sports Illustrated*, December 26, 1960, called The Soft American, which warned against the negative aspects becoming unfit in a changing world where automation and increased leisure time replaced the benefits of exercise and hard work.

President Kennedy addressed the issue of physical fitness frequently in his public pronouncements and assigned new projects to the President's Council on Physical Fitness and Sports, an organization established by Kennedy's predecessor Eisenhower on July 16, 1956. Perhaps Kennedy's most famous intervention in the area of fitness, and an indicator of the extent to which the Council became identified with him, was the fifty-mile march. (Wikipedia)

After reading about President Kennedy's challenge, two other scouts and I decided to answer the call and began planning our 50-mile hike. Together we made the decision to walk to Aurora, Illinois and back following US Route 30. I am not sure why we selected that as our route other than someone must have calculated it was around 25 miles from home. During our planning we estimated it would take us about 16 hours to complete the round-trip march of 50 miles, so we set a very early departure time. My day began when a friend arrived at my house at 4:00 am and then together we walked to the third marcher's home from where we would begin our journey in earnest. Everything went as planned until we reached the home of the third marcher. He was not outside waiting as expected and there were no signs of life in the house. We didn't want to wake his parents so we selected small pieces of gravel from the roadside and threw them at what we thought was his bedroom window. Almost immediately, a light illuminated the inside of the house. We optimistically believed we would be on our way in short order. The front door of the house slowly opened, but rather than our friend peeking out, it was his father who said, "Get out of here, he's not going!" We both looked at each other in disbelief and scurried down the street. We did some soul searching and asked each other if we were still going to do this. Then, with a sense of adventure, we agreed to carry on. Our first destination was downtown Joliet and the offices of the Joliet Herald-News. I had prepared a note, our version of a press release, to let the newspaper staff know we were embarking on a Kennedy march and that we would stop by on our return, thinking they would want to feature a story alongside a photo of the two intrepid marchers on the front cover of the paper. I stuffed my note through a mail slot located on one of the building doors and then, filled with anticipation, we began our long and hopefully fun march. Our chosen route took us along a two-lane highway, Route 30, which was the first transcontinental road to span the United States. Rather than concern ourselves with the historical significance of our selected route we were more concerned about not getting run over by a vehicle. We walked on the road's gravel shoulder, dodging approaching cars, or through the grass and weeds of the roadside shallow ditch, trying to avoid a twisted ankle caused by stepping on discarded bottles and cans. We were in high spirits as we arrived at the first major milestone on our march, the city of Plainfield, which meant we had marched 12 miles. It was about this time when my hiking partner started to complain about soreness in one of his knees. I thought nothing of it, for we were young, healthy lads. Soon he started to limp which caused me to wonder if this was a ploy to get us to reverse our course. He could tell that wasn't going to happen when he discussed the possibility with me, for I possessed a dogged determination to see the march through to the end. He had three options to get home – walk, hitchhike, or catch a bus back to Joliet. He opted for the third choice. Earlier in the morning the Bluebird bus passed us on its way to Aurora. We believed it would be making the return trip soon so we scanned the horizon and the oncoming traffic for signs of the bus. When we saw it approaching we waved our hands frantically to get the driver's attention. When the bus pulled to a halt, my lone hiking partner climbed on and without looking back left me on the shoulder of the highway to continue the march on my own. Stubbornness is one of my traits with positive and negative implications for those around me. Determined to finish what had been started, I continued on my way without him. After all, we had left a note at the Joliet

A HANDFUL OF WORM POOP

Herald-News stating our objective. By mid-morning the city of Aurora welcome sign was in view and I sought out a place of refuge for lunch and a short rest. A burger and fries, with a Coke chaser, were ordered and eaten at a small café before making the turn to begin the banter-less lonely march home.

Lunch and the short rest it provided recharged me and buoyed my confidence. It was a long slog back along the same route, but by late afternoon I was in downtown Joliet. I went directly to the Herald-News and mentioned my name and the note left early that morning. They looked puzzled and said, "What note?" With tears welling up in my eyes I explained what had just occurred and, possibly out of sympathy rather than excitement, they sent a junior reporter down who jotted a few notes about my achievement. I walked the last two miles home and collapsed on the couch. I was completely and utterly spent. The next day I could barely walk but had good reason for it. The story of my epic march did make the Herald-News but not on the front page. Buried somewhere in the paper a few days later was a two-inch-square box that contained a story about a kid who marched from Joliet to Aurora and back. I had finally discovered the sport I was good at – walking!

Experiences like long, grueling hikes and teenage jobs highlighted the route to adulthood and equipped me for a lifetime of work. They prepared, or maybe even programmed me, to be a good, loyal, and productive employee.

Chorizo Opened the Door to the World

Exposure to other cultures was a critical part of my development as a person who is both accepting of others and aware of the struggles they may have faced in life. When my family relocated to Joliet we moved into a home owned by my grandfather. It was located at 500 Francis Street on the East side of Joliet. Joliet was a city of sides. People would reference sections of the city as the East, South or West side. I rarely heard anybody refer to someone who lived on the North side of Joliet – probably because at the North end of town was the state-run Collins Street prison! Joliet was a small version of the United States – a melting pot for the immigrants of the world. It was a blue-collar town and the East side is where many immigrants started their new lives before improving their social status and making the move to the more affluent far West side. Waves of immigrants have been the life blood of our country and Joliet. It is a never-ending, familiar story as immigrants arrive in different waves of migration. No matter what country they departed from, they all had the exact same objective upon their arrival in the United States. They were seeking a better life for themselves and their families. One common trait they possessed is that they were clannish – they stuck together for comfort and security by living in the same, sometimes run-down neighborhoods. Together they built churches and social centers to preserve their heritage. Their inability to speak English caused others to ridicule and make fun of them. Their children, who were uprooted and moved to a new country where they were not readily accepted by other children, struggled to fit in and sometimes rebelled. The immigrants worked extremely hard, often performing difficult manual labor, while struggling to fit into a new society different from the one they left. Then as the years passed, their children, who struggled when younger, eventually settled down and realized they wanted it even better for their children. As their income level increased, they began to improve and renovate their homes and watch their children go off to colleges and universities. Then as the original immigrants, like my grandparents in Joliet, age and approach retirement, they watch their grandchildren live the dream they had for their children when they first arrived in this country. It is this third generation of people, like me, that more easily assimilate into society. Language is no longer an issue, they see the value of education, they qualify for and hold better jobs that, in turn, allow them to become main-stream Americans and move to more affluent neighborhoods. The old churches and social societies of their grandparents close and are shuttered while the neighborhood is turned over to a new surge of immigrants. This is exactly what happened on the East side of Joliet with the wave of Mexican immigrants who started to arrive in a trickle during my childhood. The East side of Joliet, when our family arrived in the mid-fifties, was occupied by my parents' generation. My grandparents and their peers were now the old men and women of the neighborhood. Through their thick glasses and cataracts, they observed a new wave of immigrants from Mexico begin to inhabit the neighborhoods they had helped to build. Then over the next

10-15 years, as the older eastern European residents moved to the more affluent West side or died, the East side of Joliet became predominantly Mexican. Some of their struggling children formed gangs and the neighborhood went through some very tumultuous years. But now as you ride through this area and observe the Mexican businesses that line Collins Street you can see and almost feel the stability returning to the East side. What has happened there is the same thing that happens over and over and over in immigrant neighborhoods. The East side of Joliet is an immigration story case study that reflects what my ancestors went through after their arrival in this country. That is why I am accepting of immigrants and intolerant of those who are not, for if I look honestly into an immigrant's eyes I see my grandparents. I see them longing for acceptance – nothing more. Moving to and living on the East side of Joliet helped me to understand and appreciate my grandparents story even though I did not get to know them as individuals.

Within a mile of our house were three Catholic churches – each one built by a different ethnic group. These churches helped to preserve the cultural heritage of their parishioners. The first was a Byzantine Catholic Church, Saint Mary's Assumption, where my grandparents, who were part of an ethnic minority in their eastern European homeland, had attended services. The second was a Polish Church, Saint Thaddeus, where my four cousins, who lived in a house next door, went to church and school. The third was a Slovak Church, SS. Cyril and Methodius, and it is where our family, excluding my father who grew up attending a Presbyterian church, attended mass and my siblings and I went to grade school.

In addition to churches there were many small grocery stores, taverns, and three fraternal organizations located in our neighborhood. Taverns were a fixture on the East side. There were four within a two-block radius of our house. When they first opened decades earlier, their clientele was probably divided by their ethnicity. I can imagine a Polish tavern in which everyone spoke Polish as they downed their drinks, maybe even a boilermaker with a raw egg dropped into the beer, after a long, hard day at the local steel mill. Since my father frequented a tavern daily, visiting him there often meant a treat like a candy bar, a bag of chips, or a bottle of pop. If offered a treat, the stale beer and cigarette smoke smells of the tavern quickly drove me away. Taverns seemed to have a location advantage over the small grocery stores that dotted our neighborhood for they were all located on prime real-estate – the corners. The small groceries were tucked into the middle of blocks. Their stock included the essentials like bread and milk. If a family was short on cash most of the stores offered credit by keeping a tab on what you owed – payable on the next payday. I recall occasionally running to one of the stores before school to get a loaf of bread for our school lunches and embarrassingly asking the clerk to put it on our family tab. There was still an ethnic flavor to some of the stores, which helped maintain their customer base. If you wanted Italian sausage or Italian bread, you went to Sineni's and if you wanted ground poppy seeds, to make Potica, or a loaf of fresh rye bread, you went you Kaiser's.

The fraternal organizations near my home were established decades before my arrival in Joliet and were gathering places for the different ethnicities that lived alongside each other. Along with the Slovaks and Poles, there was a strong Italian representation in our neighborhood. Though the Italian church, Saint Anthony's, was in downtown Joliet, two of the nearby fraternal organizations were Italian. I visited one of them, the Sons of Italy Club, when I was invited to a grade school graduation party for an Italian American classmate who was as cute as Annette from the Mickey Mouse Club television show. My introduction to Annette occurred while watching the Mickey Mouse Club television program in our home in Minnesota shortly after our first television was installed. I would sit in a trance and sing along as the girl of my dreams, Annette, and Bobby, my namesake, sang, "M-I-C, see you real soon, K-E-Y, why? Because

CHORIZO OPENED THE DOOR TO THE WORLD

we love you! M-O-U-S-E – Mickey Mouse!" It was exciting to get an invitation to a graduation party with both boys and girls in attendance. Like most boys my age there was a tendency to shy away from interacting with girls. My time was spent sipping on a pop while watching the cute Italian girl from a distance as if she were on television. Eventually all of the boys started clowning around and we soon discovered something that seemed a bit unusual in the rear of the building. Located there were long, dirt-filled lanes, surrounded by wooden boards, which had the shape of bowling alleys. Later I learned that these were bocce ball courts where elderly Italian men would meet to play, tell stories, drink red wine, swear, smoke small black cigars, and in general have a good time. My peek inside the club helped me to understand how they used this social gathering place to preserve their culture.

The second Italian fraternal hall belonged to the Santa Fortunata Society. The members of this organization were responsible for one of the highlights of every summer for me and my friends – The Santa Fortunata Festival. The third fraternal hall in our neighborhood was a Polish establishment. Not long after we moved to Joliet one of my older cousins married her sweetheart and the wedding reception was held in this hall. This, my first family wedding, was an exciting and memorable event. At the reception my consumption of pop exceeded my lifetime intake up to that point. When a piece of delicious, heavily frosted wedding cake was offered, it disappeared quickly. No wonder when the loud music – a mix of late-50s, early rock and roll, and polkas – began to play it caused young children like me to act crazy. My cousins and I ran around the dance floor and occasionally attempted to dance until exhaustion stopped us. When the reception began to break up we walked home in the darkness. While slowly making my way, with my ears ringing from the loud music, I thought about all of the fun we had. For the first time I understood the value of living near my relatives. Soon after arriving home I crawled into bed and lay there wide-eyed, waiting for the sugar high to lessen and sleep to come. It felt good to be living in Joliet.

   Neighbors who lived nearby also helped to create some of my childhood memories. An Italian immigrant family moved into a home next to ours and the mother would make the most delicious, crispy, crusted Italian rolls imaginable. The smell of them baking perfumed the air of the neighborhood and on a few occasions, she offered me one hot from the oven that had been slathered with butter. Biting into the warm, crispy, buttered roll awakened all my senses. If I had been able to speak Italian, "Delicioso" would have been shouted, for they certainly were. Awareness of some other Italian families that lived nearby occurred while delivering newspapers to an apartment building. Taped on a few of the apartment doors were little cut out newspaper photographs of Perry Como and Dean Martin. They were obviously proud of their Italian heritage and these two countrymen who had made something of themselves. Another indicator of their Italian heritage was in the yard next to the building. Located there in the winter was a large mound of dirt and organic material covered by canvas tarps. In the spring an elderly Italian man would remove the tarps and slowly unearth the permanently bent fig tree he had buried the previous fall. As the warm weather of spring arrived the stooped tree slowly came back to life. The leaves, which were identical to those that covered Adam and Eve's naughty bits, soon covered the tree and visually transported the elderly gardener back to Italy where fig trees are as common as oak trees in the Midwest. It the late summer a few figs would ripen and then all of a sudden disappear. Imagining the smile on the gardener's face as he savored the sweet fruit made me smile. He nurtured and cared for this tree not for the fruit but for the connection to his past. He, like all immigrants, struggled to fit into a new place while clinging to a small reminder of his past. Thanks to him I was one of the few kids in Joliet who could identify a fig tree.

   Not all my experiences with neighbors were this pleasant. In another house two doors down from ours were two elderly sisters

CHORIZO OPENED THE DOOR TO THE WORLD

who had never married. I heard others call them spinsters and I wasn't sure what that meant, but it didn't sound nice. They had little tolerance for us kids if we infringed on their property so we tended to stay clear of their house. About this time my cousin and I were begging our mothers ceaselessly for BB guns. You know, the Red Rider carbine that is referenced ("You'll shoot your eye out!") in the Hollywood movie *A Christmas Story*. Our unrelenting pleading paid off, for under both of our Christmas trees appeared the gun of our dreams. We couldn't wait to shoot our new rifles, so before the winter weather broke we were on my back porch shooting at bottle caps that we positioned on the limestone sidewalk below us. If we had paid more attention in our math classes we might have calculated the BBs' angles of trajectory after they hit the limestone. Apparently when we missed the bottle caps some of the BBs ricocheted off the sidewalk at just the perfect angle to allegedly break a window or two in the spinsters', I mean elderly ladies', back porch. We of course both denied any responsibility. Our stuttering defense fell on deaf ears for our guns were confiscated and disappeared like Jimmy Hoffa. Little did we know our eyes would be okay, but we would shoot the windows out!

It was about this time when a Mexican family moved into a home across the street from Heggie Park. One of their sons was the same age as my friends and I, so he was quickly welcomed into our neighborhood gang. When visiting their home, I occasionally observed his mother making tortillas by skillfully patting a lump of dough with her hands until it formed a thin round that she would slide onto a hot skillet surface. After a minute or so she flipped the tortilla over and it puffed up, filling the air with the smell of fresh bread. More than once she offered me one directly from the skillet that had been spread with butter and given a light sprinkling of salt. Those tortillas, my first Mexican food, were warming and delicious.

While in high school, my interest in food as a cultural access path started when this same friend staffed his uncle's Mexican food store during the summer. It was this store, the first Mexican grocery store on the East side, which sparked the romance that became a lifelong love of cooking foods from around the world. The store contained unique and exotic food items that were all new to me. There were shelves of canned goods with labels I couldn't read, fresh cactus leaves, and numerous fresh and dried chilies with unpronounceable names. The alluring smells created a feeling of adventure whenever I entered. The aroma of the carnitas, hunks of pork cooked in a cauldron of simmering pork fat in a back room, lingered in the air to combine with the scent of fresh corn tortillas and the dried chilies. Before the summer ended, my kitchen experimentation began by sautéing chorizo sausage and adding it to scrambled eggs. Wrapped in fresh, warmed, corn tortillas, this spicy concoction opened the door to a new world. My mother's standard meals, which generally consisted of a meat, potatoes, and a canned vegetable, now seemed obsolete.

My long-standing love for anything sweet was reinforced at least twice a week when a delivery truck would unload trays of fresh pastries. I learned to love a Mexican sweetbread called a "concha" and a lightly flavored molasses cookie that was shaped like a pig. The conchas were a light, airy round of sweet bread topped with a colorful, patterned swirl of a soft, cookie-like dough. All of the hours spent in this store helped me understand that learning about and eating foods from other countries and cultures can open the door to the rest of the world. It became obvious to me that anyone can begin to understand another culture if he or she gets to know that culture's food. Mexico was my port of entry and since that first experience, I have traveled the whole world through food experiences. Whenever a new ethnic grocery store is discovered, I roam the aisles, as if it were a library, seeking information about the new cuisine and culture. That East side Mexican grocery store, El Centenario, was more than just a source of Mexican food – it was an education center. There I learned that to truly understand others I must learn about the inextricable connection between them and their cuisine. That understanding has allowed me to initiate conversations with individuals from anywhere in the world by using food as my entry point. Simply asking someone about a favorite holiday food allows them to name the dish. As they joyfully describe it their eyes will light up and sparkle as they recall eating and sharing it with family. As the conversation between the two of us continues, bonds are developed that did not, nor would not, exist were it not for my knowledge of food.

I wish my grade school teachers, the nuns, would have organized field trips to ethnic grocery stores rather than religious films. They could have helped us to begin to better understanding the world and the diverse cross-section of people who populate it. Living part of my childhood in an ethnically diverse neighborhood was good for me. It helped me to understand others as different and yet the same.

Another opportunity to interact with the newly arriving Mexican immigrants, who were settling on the East side of Joliet, occurred when we all frequented a pool hall, owned and operated by Santos Garcia and Sons, which opened on Collins Street. Despite a language barrier, since their English was limited and my initial high-school Spanish class had left me confused rather than fluent, we communicated using the only word of Spanish required to begin a new game of pool, "bolas." My friends and I learned to play eight-ball, nine-ball, and straight pool by laying a quarter on the edge of the pool table and shouting, "bolas." Santos or one of his sons would rack the game of our choice and then as he departed, use one finger to deftly slide the quarter from the edge of the table into the palm of his other hand. We spent many hours there honing both our pool and bullshitting skills. While some took their skills to the bars around Joliet, my foundational pool skills were further developed while serving in the Air Force. All squadron housing common areas had a pool table. The rules were simple – if you won, you continued to play; if you lost, you had to wait your turn to try and win. During my four years of service my skills grew and a few years after my discharge I purchased my own pool table. This came about when my older sister called to tell me a friend's mother, who had lost her spouse of many years, wanted to sell a vintage pool table located in her basement. When I made the trip to view the table the owner shared a few stories about her deceased husband. One related to a very distinct and odd pool cue. Her husband had taken a wooden cue and cut off a one foot length from both the top and bottom. He then fit and inserted these cut ends into a piece of pipe that had been shaped into a large "U" shape. The cue with the "U" in the middle was used to make shots when a basement support column, next to the pool table, got in the way of aligning the shot. With a twinkle in her eye she noted her husband had told anyone who would listen that the special cue stick was crafted for heavy chested women. Good stories can last a lifetime, or even longer, if we have storytellers to pass them on.

My exposure to other cultures increased after joining the Air Force and completing basic training. It was a cultural immersion experience, for my training flight was made up of people of different races and from different parts of the country. For instance, the experience of standing naked next to an African-American man didn't occur until I stepped into an open bay shower with about 15 other naked young men in basic training. It was obvious he had never showered next to a white man because as we stood drying ourselves off he asked if he could feel the small spikes of hair starting to emerge from my shaved head. He slowly rubbed the top of my head before my turn at rubbing the top of his head. This resulted in a good laugh for us both. In basic training, we were expected to lose our identities and just be "airmen" who responded quickly and without question when ordered to do anything. Our heads had been shaved and we wore identical clothing, yet our skin color and regional accents, the things that could have categorized us, didn't. Instead, we all marched to the same cadence and were united together by a common fear of our drill instructor. The prejudices and misconceptions of others we each brought with us were temporarily erased from our thoughts as we shouted, "Yes Sir," and marched our way through basic training. Yet, being exposed to individuals who were different in many ways from me would have been an education missed had I not joined the military.

Despite the expected harshness and rigor of basic training, the sense of personal freedom and independence developed and felt during my childhood allowed me to leave home for basic training without emotion or a great sense of loss or longing. Following basic training, we were granted a leave, allowing me to spend a week back home prior to reporting to my new duty station in Louisiana. Soon after my arrival home, the feeling that I didn't belong there any more overcame me. Enlisting in the military had gotten me out of my crowded family home and the chaos that sometimes existed there. My life, at this juncture, now had a clear defined path forward. Nothing held me back when the week of leave ended. My outlook and attitude regarding what home meant had been redefined.

The opportunity to request overseas duty occurred one year into my four-year enlistment while stationed at Barksdale Air Force Base in Shreveport, Louisiana. My recruiter had promised me the opportunity to see the world and it turned out to be true. The process started by going to the squadron office and reviewing a binder that contained a list of all possible overseas assignment locations. While completing the request form, which required me to list three choices, it caused me to recall the form completed with the recruiter regarding my military job training choices. Those choices were meaningless for the military assigned me where they needed me. My current concern was I would select three countries and then the Air Force would just ship me to Vietnam. My first choice was Clark Airbase in the Philippines. It seemed remotely attractive because it was far away, tropical and it was not Vietnam. To my amazement, the Air Force gave me what I had requested about five months later. I received orders to report for duty in the Philippines.

A leave at home was scheduled before my departure for the Philippines and once again I felt out of place. Attachments like friends, who had gone off to college, the military or who worked 40-hour-a-week jobs, were not around; my old friends had moved on with their lives. The time between high school and adulthood is a time of transition; a period when my age denied me the right to reminisce and long for the past. My challenge was to look forward while discovering and defining "me" in the adult world that lay ahead. I departed home without fanfare and flew to visit a military friend in California before departing for the Philippines. The highlight of my weekend visit was seeing San Francisco and walking around Haight-Ashbury where the smell of weed perfumed the air. This section of San Francisco, the hippy culture capital of the world, caused me to quickly feel out of place. As we walked around this city, where the "summer of love" had taken place just months before, I watched small groups of hippies hanging out in Golden Gate Park and felt a twinge of envy. Eighteen months earlier, my long hair and attitude might have lead me down the road to hippy town, but my trip had been detoured by the draft board. My military-length haircut and plain clothing caused me to now feel out of place. Without much thought, I quickly accepted the fact that I was just a tourist longing to be a local and moved on with my life.

 The 20-hour journey to the Philippines was long and tiring. In between long expanses of the Pacific Ocean, the plane stopped to refuel in Hawaii and then Guam before it finally touched down at Clark Airbase. Like one of the hundreds of legalized prostitutes who resided outside the gates of Clark Airbase, the tropical heat and humidity wrapped warmly around me as I exited the plane. The Asian features of the Filipinos and the lush, tropical landscape, including a large, inactive volcano looming in the near distance, confirmed the fact that this was a different side of the world. After being processed in and assigned my place in a barracks I went to the Base Exchange to get something to eat. A huge plate of fried rice and a copy of the Stars and Stripes newspaper helped relieve my jet-lag stupor. The paper's cover photo, which showed soldiers in combat in Vietnam, reinforced the point that the deadly fighting was now much closer. I felt excited and uneasy at the same time.

It didn't take long for me to settle into the routine of work, for the work was very much the same here as it was in Louisiana. Common interests or organizations, like a person's place of work, often define our social circles and that was the case for me. The friends I made and hung out with during my non-working hours were mainly people who worked the afternoon shift with me. Working this shift allowed me to avoid both the heat of mid-day and the potential hassles of dealing with the leadership of our work unit. Working on the flight line and being around military aircraft always intrigued me. A plane taking off, especially a fighter jet, would cause me to stop what I was doing and just watch in amazement as it hurled down the runway before rocketing into the air, followed almost instantly by the time-lagged roar of its jet engines. In addition to fueling military aircraft, the dispatcher often sent me to refuel commercial planes. So many troops were being transported to and from Vietnam by this time in the war that the military had contracted with commercial carriers to fly troops back and forth. It seemed kind of crazy to be refueling a Continental Airlines 707 on an airbase in the Philippines. The attraction of refueling these commercial planes was the stewardesses. They often stood by the open galley door allowing me to gawk at them and their pretty legs from down below. Starting a conversation might result in a treat from home. If the plane had departed from the US, they would occasionally throw me a carton of fresh whole milk if asked. While waiting for the lengthy refueling process to finish, the soldiers sitting above me in the plane often occupied my thoughts. The draft boards knew no prejudice when they filled their quotas, so it was certain the planes passengers reflected a multi-cultural mix that mirrored my own work shift diversity. Fear and happiness are universally felt no matter what your race. Depending on the destination of the plane, I imagined the common fear and uncertainty felt by those going to Vietnam and the immense happiness and relief of those who were heading home physically intact, though probably mentally scared. The cargo on other planes placed the sorrow and immense sadness of the Vietnam War right in front of my face. On more than one occasion when sent out to refuel large C-141 cargo planes, the rear loading door would be wide open. In those open cargo bays were neatly arranged rows of flag-draped caskets, filled with the remains of soldiers who had died in the jungles of Vietnam. All the military ground crew working on these planes did so reverently. Voices were kept low and our faces reflected a true sense of sadness as we went about our work to prepare the plane for the next leg of the gloomy journey. I felt sad and angry. This startling and grim reality validated that holding a fuel nozzle was preferable to an M-16 rifle. My decision to enlist, rather than wait to be drafted, was a good one.

 I enjoyed working the afternoon shift, as it was a cooler and calmer part of the day. Once the tropical sun had set, darkness and the large lights that lined the flight line attracted both common and unique bugs. At times, huge insects we called rice bugs, as well as hordes of crickets, would be so thick on the flight line that as my fuel truck's tires crushed them it was audible in the cab. Since the truck was full of explosive jet fuel, whenever a lightning storm was within a three-mile radius of the airbase all refueling operations were to be stopped. On one occasion, just after the sun had set, I was standing on atop the truck at the refill terminal holding the release lever that allowed the fuel to flow through a large fill pipe and into my truck's empty tank. While standing there day dreaming a bolt of lightning illuminated my surroundings as it struck and broke a telephone pole about 40 yards from my truck. This caused me to quickly spring from the top of the truck and call the dispatcher. With a jittery and nervous voice, he was informed that a trip to the barracks to change my underwear would be necessary before another plane could be fueled. When our shift ended at 11:00 pm we would all head to "midnight chow." This was a breakfast meal we considered a workday ritual. Challenges to eat a dozen eggs or drink a small juice glass half filled with Tabasco sauce were offered and accepted. On Friday, we bypassed this meal, for like everyone else in the working world, we waited for Friday and the end of our work week.

Staying on the airbase kept me in a Western world and protected me from the third-world conditions that existed in most of the Philippines. Walking down the main commercial street in Angeles City, which was located just outside of the airbase, was literally and figuratively a world away from Collins Street and the eastside of Joliet. The storefronts were more like huts than buildings. Rather than visit stores to purchase clothing or shoes, the shop owners would take your measurements and then make custom apparel and shoes. It wasn't long before my custom-made, military-green fatigues and matching work-hat were ready for pickup. The fatigues, unlike their baggy, military-issue counterparts, were form-fitting. Embroidered on one side of my unique hat was the word "Chick," my childhood nickname, and on the other side "Haight-Ashbury" surrounded by embroidered flowers. This flower-power symbol was my mini-protest against the war.

Angeles City looked much better, but smelled the same, at night. Although there were evening entertainment options on the airbase, including a large airman's club where I could listen to live jazz and sip a glass of scotch, my friends and I often headed for the raunchy bars in town. All the bars had two things in common. The first was prostitutes who wore photo IDs that signified they were "clean." These supposedly inspected and clean prostitutes were intended to ensure you did not need a visit to a doctor and a prescription for penicillin a week after a romp. Secondly, all of the bars had rock and roll music blaring and many of the bars featured live music. The live music, rather than the prostitutes, is what attracted me to town. Within a few weeks of a new album being released by popular rock and roll artists, the local bands would be playing and singing perfect versions of the hits they contained. The bands were so good that if I closed my eyes it was easy to imagine being at a live concert listening to the Beatles, Jimi Hendrix, or Led Zeppelin. After a night on the town we would walk back toward the main gate while hawkers shouted, "hot bread" and "balut." I often bought and enjoyed the warm, satisfying, sweet bread rolls, but never summoned up the courage to eat a duck egg that contained an almost-fully-formed duck embryo. These visits to town and other excursions around the Philippines helped me view the world differently.

On a few weekends, friends and I took the train into Manila or north of the base to a beach resort. Once, while in Manila, we arranged to have a motorized outrigger canoe take us to Corregidor Island. This island played a crucial role when the Americans liberated the Philippines during World War II by driving out the Japanese. Walking among the ruins of former buildings and gun embankments triggered me to think of the American soldiers who had fought there less than 25 years earlier. Not many days later, while walking through the Manila American Cemetery, the 17,000 white marble grave markers fully explained the cost they had paid. I had never felt so overwhelmed with sadness.

On another occasion, we took a train in the opposite direction from Manila to get to a small resort on a stretch of undeveloped beach. The resort building, a modest, single-story structure that had the look of a 1950s motel back in the States, sat alone on an uninhabited, palm-tree-lined, white-sand beach. All that was visible, in either direction, was white-sand beaches and palm trees – no other buildings or people. Compared to filthy Angeles City, where we had boarded the train, this was a paradise. We spent most of our time walking on or just lazing on the beach. As we walked we found beautiful sea shells and the occasional corroded, World-War-II bullet littering the beach. We were told this beach, along the Lingayen Gulf, was one of the landing beaches used by General McArthur's US Forces when they retook the Philippines from the Japanese in 1945. On one occasion, we hired an outrigger canoe to take us out to some nearby reefs to snorkel. This was a rudimentary, hand-crafted boat with a small gas engine and bamboo outriggers. As the small craft glided over the crystal-clear water's smooth surface, I sat transfixed in the bow while watching flying fish repeatedly break the surface, glide a short distance, and then disappear into the clear blue water. As they flew the sun reflected off their translucent wings, which created small, rainbow bands of color. When the boat slowed above the reefs I cautiously climbed out and clung onto the boat's outriggers while observing the reefs and the sea life below. When the boat headed back to the unspoiled beach I felt fortunate to be experiencing this magical natural setting. My weekend in this tropical paradise helped me understand that most of the Philippine Islands differed from Angeles City. It was a country of touching natural beauty. Getting away from the airbase also gave me an altered view of the Filipino people. The airbase and the wealth it brought to the poor country, attracted hucksters and con men from wide and far. They were in your face as soon as you walked out of the airbase gate. Away from the base the people were kind, helpful, and wonderful to be around. The airbase not only spoiled the natural beauty of the county, it tainted many of the people who lived near it.

Many Filipino men worked on the air base, and those jobs were sought after because the wages surpassed what could be earned off the base. The jobs they performed were the non-technical, manual-labor jobs such as landscaping, painting, and housekeeping. In my POL (Petroleum, Oil, and Lubricants) work area I would often see these men laboring under the hot tropical sun with rags covering their heads. They were all skinny, taut as a rubber band and worked hard. At lunch time, they would gather in a circle under the shade of a nearby tree, and open their banana-leaf-wrapped food packets and set them on the ground in front of themselves. Then while squatting down, rather than sitting, they would tuck into their lunch of rice and fish using their fingers as utensils while chatting in their native language.

While I watched them with an honest interest, modern aircraft taxied by in the background, helping me recognize that we were from two different worlds. That sentiment was reinforced a few months later when Neil Armstrong stepped onto the surface of the moon.

One of the benefits of serving in the military in a third-world country was that the common military chores such as cleaning the barracks, cutting the lawns or being assigned to mess hall duty were performed by local labor. So for five dollars per week, a shared house boy would do my laundry, make my bed, shine my shoes, and clean the barracks. The house boy, who was really a man, did a great job and made my life a pretty easy one. I worked 40 hours per week, had weekends off, and was responsible for little else. Just at the time Neil Armstrong landed his spacecraft upon the surface of the moon, my house boy came walking by. As we huddled around a small, black-and-white television watching that historic moment with awe on our faces, we invited him to join us. We quickly and excitedly explained what was happening. As Neil Armstrong exited the landing craft and stepped onto the surface of the moon, the house boy said it could not be true. He could not, nor would he believe someone was stepping onto the surface of the moon no matter what was said to try and convince him. He lacked the understanding to accept the fact that was right in front of him. Expecting him to think like me was unrealistic. He, in essence, came from a different side of the moon with a completely different view of the world.

After my 18 months of duty in the Philippines, there were still seven months of my four- year enlistment to be served. This was in late 1969 and the government had begun to cut back on the war effort in Vietnam and military spending in general. They began to give "early outs," or early discharges, to some military personnel. While hoping they would discharge me and send me home rather than to another military installation, I received orders to report to an airbase located in Duluth, Minnesota.

The mid-September weather was fantastic when I arrived in

CHORIZO OPENED THE DOOR TO THE WORLD

Duluth. After 18 months of tropical heat and humidity, this was a refreshing and welcome change. Soon after a new friend and I bought fishing poles, we rented a boat and found ourselves sitting in the middle of Fish Lake under clear blue skies. All the hardwood trees surrounding this northern lake were covered in leaves that were varying shades of orange, yellow, red, and brown. The calm water along the shores of the lake reflected the colorful trees creating a mirror image that was stunningly beauty. After spending the next three hours drifting and fishing, one of us finally hooked and landed a fish. We promptly threw it back so officials wouldn't have to change the name of the lake. Three months later, when the wind chill was 70 degrees below zero, I was out refueling a fighter plane, wearing a fur-lined hooded parka and inflatable rubber boots, longing for the tropics. At this point I was a "short timer," for just a few months remained on my four-year enlistment. I was eager to get out and get on with my life.

A few weeks later my "early out" became reality when I was notified my discharge would occur two months early. To begin the process of my liberation, my discharge papers we picked up from the base headquarters office. It was quickly noted that a smartass clerk, who had typed up the discharge form, misspelled my home town of Joliet. Before handing a copy to anyone, the "T" had to be crossed out and replaced with a "J." Within a few days I traveled home to Joliet to begin the next phase of my life.

Serving in the military was beneficial in many ways, but the most important was the exposure to the people different than me. I served with people from all over the United States who were like and unlike me. The US is often referred to as a melting pot of immigrants, and my military units reflected that same hodge-podge society. Our similarities were based on the fact that we were all humans and were serving in the military. The dissimilarities stemmed from our differing backgrounds. Our personal histories – where and how we were raised, our families' social standings, and our ethnicities – were the building blocks that both formed us and differentiated us. Having to fit in and communicate with an endless variety of people was a great experience for me. It helped me understand people and accept those who are unlike me.

Before the military, as an 18-year-old, I certainly lacked direction. My parents could not be accused of trying to control my actions, for little, if any, advice or direction was given by them. A simple desire to work, make money, and move out of the family home is what drove me until my enlistment. Looking back, my time in the military, and the structure it provided, may have been the best thing for me at that time. As a young adult, without any clear direction in life, who knows what I would have done and where I would have ended up. My guess is I would have been an honest-to-goodness hippy for some period, worked, and gotten married. Following that conventional path would have meant I would have missed out on the exposure to, and the acceptance of, the broader physical and cultural world my military experience provided. That four-year escape from Joliet changed me for the better.

And Here's the Beatles

Come mothers and fathers
Throughout the land
And don't criticize
What you can't understand
Your sons and your daughters
Are beyond your command
—Bob Dylan, The Times They Are a-Changin'

The nineteen sixties were a stimulating time to be a teenager. New generations have always sought ways to separate themselves from the previous one and the rebellious baby boomers found many ways to express their uniqueness and independence. The last five years of the sixties were a time of unrestrained, counter-cultural change. This is when hippies became hip and our clothing, hairstyles, and music spearheaded a rebellion against both the middle-class lifestyles and values of our parents' generation. This cultural phenomenon, combined with the age-old desire for independence from both parents and home that almost all teenagers seek, made our generation distinct.

The rock and roll music of the sixties became both a

generational anthem and a long-enduring symbol of our generation. As a young child, my parents' music played in the background on a kitchen radio that was always tuned into the local Joliet radio station—WJOL. Big bands and crooners like Frank Sinatra and Dean Martin dominated the station's playlist until the mid-fifties when things began to change. While an older cousin and her friends were listening to Elvis Presley and other early rock and roll musicians in the early sixties, my interest in music just began to stir. At that time there were two devices that allowed me to listen to music on my own, one of which was a crystal radio:

A crystal radio receiver, also called a crystal set or cat's whisker receiver, is a very simple radio receiver, popular in the early days of radio. It needs no other power source but that received solely from the power of radio waves received by a wire antenna. It gets its name from its most important component, known as a crystal detector, originally made from a piece of crystalline mineral such as galena. This component is now called a diode.

Crystal radios are the simplest type of radio receiver and can be made with a few inexpensive parts, such as a wire for an antenna, a coil of copper wire for adjustment, a capacitor, a crystal detector, and earphones. They are distinct from ordinary radios as they are passive receivers, while other radios use a separate source of electric power such as a battery or the mains power to amplify the weak radio signal so as to make it louder. Thus, crystal sets produce rather weak sound and must be listened to with sensitive earphones, and can only receive stations within a limited range. (Wikipedia)

I very clearly remember lying in bed at night with my crystal radio. Tuning the small device to find a station with enough power, so that the signal would not fade in and out, was a challenge that could last for hours. Adjusting the tuning dial, which was miniscule and finicky, required the touch of a brain surgeon. While listening through a small earbud and holding my breath, the dial would be rotated the distance of a human hair.

AND HERE'S THE BEATLES

Occasionally through the hiss and buzzing, a faint voice or some music that always sounded like it came from far away, would be heard. The listening experience remembered most was when a station from somewhere in northern Iowa, that broadcast the newly franchised Minnesota Twins baseball games, was tuned in. Since my early childhood had been spent in Minnesota I had a natural affinity for the Twins. It felt dreamlike to be laying in the darkness and listening to that very faint, wavering signal while the on-field exploits of players Harmon Killebrew, Bob Allison, Zoilo Versalles and Tony Oliva caused the announcer's voice to crackle with excitement. That little, mystical device allowed me to listen to games played far away in the state of Minnesota, and because of that experience that was the only time that professional baseball meant anything to me. It seems insignificant now but at the time it was as magical as the first viewing of a television.

Another device used to listen to music was a battery-powered transistor radio. It was a small, rectangular device with two knobs, one for the volume control and the other for tuning the radio. It had a carrying loop near the top so the radio could hang from my wrist. The competition with my siblings to gain access to the radio and dead batteries meant this shared entertainment device rarely entertained me.

At about age fourteen, I developed a true interest in music and it lead to the purchase of a record player. The record player had the appearance of a small suitcase that, when opened, revealed a turntable located on the bottom half and the speakers built into the lid. After purchasing it at a local discount store and lugging it home, I opened the lid, put on a record and listened while in a trance-like state. Sitting there motionless, with my head no more than 12 inches from the speakers, while listening to high-fidelity sounds, made the music from all the radios I had ever listened to sound garbled and obsolete. This experience caused me to fall head-over-heels in love with early rock and roll music. At that time, vinyl records were the most popular and readily available form of recorded music, and I was ready to start collecting.

To build my record collection, I visited the Polk Brothers' store in downtown Joliet, as it had a large inventory of records. Records were organized by genre and the alphabet to help customers locate their favorite artists. My musical tastes had not yet fully developed so most of my time was spent just flipping through the albums and looking at the cover artwork. My early purchases included music by the Everly Brothers, Roy Orbison, Buddy Holly and the Beach Boys. Sitting at our dining room table, I would listen to their songs play over and over again. The music and the words of the songs spoke to me. Rote repetition taught me the words to all the songs, which came in handy a few years later while stationed in Shreveport, Louisiana. A friend and I, fueled by a few drinks, would loudly sing along with the Everly Brothers as they played on the juke box at the Satellite Lounge. It was an early attempt at karaoke. The music of these artists, which has stood the test of time, helped to pave the way for the rock and roll explosion that would happen during the next few years. Rock and roll was indeed here to stay.

I still have around 300 vinyl LP records in a front hall closet and they are a visible chronological history of my changing taste in music. Bob Dylan, the Beatles, the Rolling Stones, Jimi Hendrix, The Byrds, Led Zeppelin, Buffalo Springfield, James Taylor, and Crosby, Stills, Nash and Young were all favorites from the mid-sixties to the early seventies. A few years ago I walked into a record store in Chicago that featured old vinyl records. While flipping through the bins, some of the records that were in my collection began to appear. Some of them had some real value based on the marked prices. That visit caused me to pull my albums out of the closet to assess my collection a few days later. Using sticky-backed notepaper, I alphabetized the records in stacks on the floor and then listed them on a spreadsheet by artist and album title. Each album brought memories of not just the music, but of places, people, events, and specific periods of my life. For instance, the Bob Dylan song "Girl from the North Country" was on the Nashville Skyline album purchased in 1969

AND HERE'S THE BEATLES

while stationed on an Air Force base in Duluth, Minnesota. As soon as the album cover was in view it caused me to recall that song, which then transported me back to social events with "girls from the north country" who lived in and around Duluth. When an early Led Zeppelin song is played I'm immediately conveyed back to 1968 and my barracks in the Philippines. Upon hearing Aretha Franklin, I see myself lying on my bunk in the same barracks. While lying there, in the next section of the barracks separated only by steel lockers, African American airmen played a card game called Tonk, while screaming Aretha entertained them and kept me from sleeping. Each album had a personal story attached to it, making the task of sorting the albums a magical flashback experience. As the albums were organized and stacked, an interest in their value resulted in many internet searches to see what others had paid for the same album. It turned out my vinyl records all have an intrinsic emotional value, while only a few have any real cash value. Spending a few evenings doing this was an exercise very similar to discovering an old shoebox full of photos from earlier in life. First the lid is removed from the box and then life stands still for a while as faded images from the past stir memories and emotions. It was a trip down memory lane triggered by the album cover images and the music within. When my sorting exercise was finished, the albums were returned to the closet in alphabetical order. The next time I want to go tripping down memory lane, it will be an organized adventure.

Military service caused me to miss out on the landmark late sixties rock and roll concerts, including Woodstock. My musical entertainment at that time was provided at local downtown bars in the Philippines where some amazingly talented cover bands performed songs by Jimi Hendrix, the Beatles, Cream, and The Doors. Late on Friday night, after working the afternoon shift, or on Saturday night, friends and I went off base to frequent the countless bars that lined the street leading to the base entrance. There had to be 20-30 bars in just a small area so the term "bar-hopping" clearly described what we did. While sipping glasses of scotch on the rocks, or nursing bottles of San Miguel beer, we listened to very loud psychedelic music. Once, after returning from the bars in the early morning hours and passing out in bed, I missed the experience of feeling the effects of an earthquake. I may have subconsciously believed the vibration was from the psychedelic band's music that was still buzzing in my ears. Later that morning, when others talked about running out of the barracks, I had to ask, "What earthquake?"

One of my co-workers had brought his wife to the Philippines and due to the lack of housing on the air base they rented an apartment in town. Occasionally they invited a small group of us over for a party, which allowed us to get off the base and feel like we were at a friend's house back home. Music was central to our gatherings and we kept up with the popular music of the day by purchasing albums at the Base Exchange or knock-off versions sold in town. An album by The Zombies, along with too much Mateus wine, provided the entertainment one evening. We had pooled our money and purchased a whole case of Mateus from the base Airman's Club. It was a nice change from the local beer and it fueled a night of conversation and comradery. When the party ended, it was light outside and our host, who also had a car, drove us back to the base while we were still singing songs by The Zombies:

What's your name? (What's your name?)
Who's your daddy? (Who's your daddy?)
(He rich) Is he rich like me?
Has he taken (Has he taken)
Any time (Any time)
(To show) To show you what you need to live?
—The Zombies, Time of the Season

During my four years of military service, music was a link to home and the counter-cultural revolution that was occurring. My record collection grew and my stereo equipment purchases ramped up. My purchases included a receiver, a turntable, and a large set of speakers, which were crammed into one of my two lockers in the barracks. I would often open the locker doors; put on my stereo headphones and let the likes of Led Zeppelin transport me elsewhere. My last purchase was a TEAC reel-to-reel tape player that allowed me to spend countless hours transferring music from my and others' record albums onto tape. I loved the new rock and roll music, for it made me feel part of something larger than myself. It was generational.

Not long after being discharged from the military in early 1970 I heard a band perform at a local bar. They were all talented musicians and often covered the songs of the musicians and bands that I listened to, like the Rolling Stones and the Beatles. Because of my interest in photography I often photographed the band and they ended up using a few of my photos to advertise their upcoming performances. Following the band allowed me to watch them grow and develop from just covering other band's songs to performing their own material. During that time period the band was been busy writing and recording songs after signing a recording contract for their first album. At about the same time, I became engaged and asked if they would play at my wedding reception. They made it clear they didn't normally perform at weddings, and only agreed because of our relationship. At the reception, they invited me to join them on stage to joyously singing the Beatles song "Hey Jude" at the top of my lungs. The next day the band packed up and headed to New York City to perform the following weekend at The Bitter End in Greenwich Village. It was their debut performance, scheduled by their new record label, to showcase their new album. My wife and I headed in the same direction at the start of our honeymoon and were sitting in the audience when they took the stage and performed later that week. It was magical watching and listening to them onstage performing their original music, which reminded me of one of my favorite bands – Crosby, Stills, Nash and Young.

I did attend one outdoor music festival. It was the Kickapoo Creek Rock festival held in Heyworth, Illinois. The immense anticipation and excitement of attending my first large outdoor music festival faded as it began and continued to rain ceaselessly all weekend until the festival site, a grassy pastureland, turned into a muddy quagmire. It was dreamlike lying in the back seat of my car while listening to the pitter patter of rain accompanying the muted, soulful blues of BB King, who was performing on the stage some distance away. Late Sunday morning, while in a sleepless trance, I packed my car and departed for home. Driving past the surreal scenes of muddy grass fields strewn with cardboard shelters, abandoned tents, camping gear, and garbage helped me realize that the hype often exceeds the actual experiences of life. The departing view from my driver's side window, including someone sleeping on an upright motorcycle, is frozen in time in a photo snapped on the way out. Not long after pulling onto the highway to start my journey home, Canned Heat's song "Going up the Country" began to play on the car radio. Since I had heard Canned Heat perform that song on stage just the day before, listening to the lyrics of the song caused some confused reflection. As noted in an online article, "Although linked to the counterculture of the 1960s' back-to-the-land movement, Wilson's lyrics are ambiguous:

Now baby pack your leaving trunk, you know we've got to leave today
Just exactly where we're going I cannot say, but we might even leave the U.S.A.
'Cause there's a brand new game that I don't wanna play" (Wikipedia)

These lyrics embody the exploration and search for direction and identity that occurred in the late sixties. Not only were the lyrics vague, so was the future course of my adult life at this point. The phrases, "just be yourself" or "I have to find myself," were used excessively as if we were all lost on our life's journey. The music and the lyrics of many of the late-sixties songs easily became the soundtrack for my late-teen and young-adult life. A time when

I both struggled to find myself and define how I'd fit into the broader world.

The clothing we wore in the sixties was another way we expressed our individuality and differentiated ourselves from our parents and their generation. Whatever clothes I wore as a child created no lasting memories, for at that time there was no fashionable clothing for young boys from blue-collar families. We were all dressed like the "Beav" in the "Leave it to Beaver" television show – plaid shirts and non-descript pants. The only feature that changed with the seasons was the length of our shirt sleeves. For me it was impossible to develop a sense of fashion or to wear clothing that made a statement. I attended Catholic schools where wearing a school uniform was required. Wearing navy-blue pants and a light blue or white shirt day after day stymied my understanding of fashion and its ability to separate you from the crowd. It didn't get any better in high school where we were required to wear a uniform that consisted of a non-descript brownish, yellowish, tannish V-neck pullover sweater. This uninteresting, colored, fuzzy sweater was made of some wonder synthetic fiber that allowed us to wear it for all four years of high school if we didn't outgrow the one we purchased our freshman year. A few cash-strapped parents were aware of this because some freshman, who obviously should have been wearing a smaller size, wore sweaters that went down to their knees and had the sleeves rolled up. In my case I hardly grew at all in high school, so my sweater graduated with me after four years. Located on one side of the sweater front was a school emblem patch. It featured a prominent tower located on top of the school building. After four years of wear and trips through the washing machine, the emblem patch appeared to be just a smudge. We all became very adept at determining a student's year of high school simply by assessing the condition of his sweater. By the time we were seniors the sweater was nothing but a mass of balled-up tense fiber. We no longer had to hang them on a hanger; we could just stand our sweater in the corner of our bedroom. After observing the priests and brothers who ran the school and taught many of the classes, the reason for wearing the same clothing day after day became clear. Since they wore the same habit day after day this was yet another recruiting scheme intended to rob of us of our independence and individuality.

If it weren't for the birth of the hippie movement and the influence of the sixties music culture, the rest of my life may have been spent in navy blue pants and light blue shirts. Maybe it was those "parochial blues" that lead us to blue jeans. Blue jeans, or more specifically Levis blue jeans, became standard wear for teens in the late 1960s. They were like the bottom half of a generational uniform. Jeans in all colors and styles replaced whatever we had worn before. Their popularity made them the universal pants of choice. In addition to blue jeans we wore colored denim, corduroy, and of course bell-bottom jeans. The act of spending my hard-earned money on a piece of clothing was frightening and caused anxiety. When a clerk approached me to ask if his assistance was required my response was always "no." I would instead continue standing in front of the clothing counters filled with a myriad of colors and styles of Levi jeans, almost paralyzed with fear. Admitting to the fact that I couldn't make a buying decision because my experience was non-existent was difficult.

The other half of the baby boomer generational uniform had to be T-shirts. That style of shirt was not new; as young children, we all wore horizontal-striped T-shirts. What was new was that this style of shirt became a message board for a generation. The first tee shirt I owned, with any type of art or printing on it, was acquired in 1966. Obtaining my very own mustard-yellow T-shirt, with the words "U.S. Air Force" printed across the front, required me to enlist in the U.S. Air Force for four years. One of my first stops on the first morning of basic training was at a storeroom where we were issued our military clothing. My first printed T-shirt, that symbol of the sixties, was included in a pile of drab green military-issue clothing. For the next four years that yellow T-shirt traveled with me, as I changed bases three more times, and then retired to one of my dresser drawers where it stayed for a few decades after my discharge. It was symbolic of both my time in the military and the decade in which T-shirts became symbols of the baby boomer generation. Being in the military from 1966-1970 meant I missed out on some of the counter-culture apparel revolution that saw T-shirts move from utilitarian work shirts into fashion statements and cultural symbols. Although I do clearly remember buying two white T-shirts with floral motif horizontal stripes across the chest, at the Clark Air Base exchange while I was stationed in the Philippines. They were surfer tees that featured a Hawaiian pattern. Being from the Midwest I was the furthest thing from a surfer dude, yet in the tropical Philippines, when I was off duty, a floral decorated tee seemed appropriate. Once I was discharged from the military, T-shirts became my top of choice during the hot summer months. From that point forward and up until today decorated tees shirts, and the message they intentionally send, are still a part of my wardrobe.

One of my boldest fashion statements was the sports jacket purchased for my high school graduation in 1964. It was a baby-blue, collarless sport jacket inspired by the Beatles. Much of the fashion revolution that occurred during the sixties was inspired by the music scene of that decade. The Beatles had a profound influence on me and my taste in music. When they appeared on the Ed Sullivan show in February of 1964, I was immediately hooked on both their look and especially their music. So, when my mother took me shopping just a few months later for a suit or sports jacket for my spring time graduation, a collarless sports jacket was my choice. Apparel fashion, if you buy into the concept of fashion, is intended to make us feel special. It has the power to make us feel distinctive and stand out from the crowd. Living on the East side of Joliet, and attending an all-boys Catholic high school on the west side, meant I did not fit into the many of the social circles, or cliques, which existed at school. Most of the students were from the more affluent West side. There were 254 students in the 1964 graduating class of Joliet Catholic High

School and I was the only one wearing a collarless sports jacket at our graduation ceremony. Standing out in the crowd made me feel special. Feeling unique is important in life and that jacket helped me understand that.

Along with our clothing, the next most radical departure from our parents' look was our hairstyles. For me it was certainly the Beatles and their flop-top look that caused me to let my hair grow and fall onto my forehead and over my ears. As the years passed and the Beatles' hairstyles continued to lengthen, so did a generation's. Barbers of our parents' generation, who had cut our hair as children had to learn, or maybe forget, some haircutting skills. Parents everywhere complained in unison about our long hair, which was often reason enough to let it grow even longer. Following this trend of wearing one's hair longer lasted until early in 1966 when, while in basic training, my mop top was shaved off, leaving only small nubs of hair sticking up from my scalp. Following the inclination to let our hair grow long was the desire to grow some sort of facial hair. When my hormones made it possible I sported a mustache while in the Air Force. Of course, there were rules that governed the length of a military-approved mustache. It could not be grown below the sides of your mouth, so growing the popular Fu-Manchu-style mustache was not a court martial offense, but reason enough to get your butt chewed. Before being discharged from the Air Force, a run-in with my unit noncommissioned officer over the length of my mustache led to a verbal reprimand. My tendency toward "hippyness" – long hair and facial hair—had been suppressed for almost four years while serving my country. With just a few weeks to go before my discharge, my mustache grew longer and was noticed by my unit's Master Sergeant.

This Master Sergeant had it in for me anyway over an incident that had occurred a few weeks earlier. My schedule at the time was working a 16-hour overnight shift and then being off duty for the next 32 hours. Along with a shift partner we would start our shift at 3:00 pm and it would end at 7:00 am the next morning.

AND HERE'S THE BEATLES

On a day when our shift would have started at 3:00 o'clock in the afternoon, the Sargent called a unit meeting for 7:00 am in the morning. My partner and I wrongly assumed it did not apply to us until the loud banging on our barrack's door awoke us from a sound sleep. We were ordered to get dressed and report for duty. When we arrived at our duty station we both received a butt chewing and were ordered to take a large refueling truck down to the motor pool car wash and wash it as punishment for our failure to follow orders. We drove the 5,000-gallon tanker truck to the motor pool only to discover the car wash was indeed only for cars. We backed the large truck into the wash bay but only about a third of the truck fit into the building. Since this was late December and I was stationed in Duluth, Minnesota, that posed a problem. It was well below freezing outside and any heat that was in the wash bay quickly dissipated. We did our best to carry out the sergeant's orders but as soon as the nozzle's water spray hit the ice-cold metal sides of the truck, it began to freeze. We continued to spray the tanker truck until it was coated in ice and there were icicles hanging from the bottom.

We then drove it back to our duty station for inspection. While biting our cheeks to keep from busting out in laughter, we sincerely told him we tried our best to wash the truck as ordered but that it was impossible to do so due to the inclement weather. When, a few weeks later, and just a week or so before my discharge date, he noticed my mustache was growing beyond the edges of my mouth, he threatened to have me thrown out of the Air Force with a dishonorable discharge, if it wasn't trimmed. Of course I said, "Yes, Sir," trimmed my mustache and waited for my discharge with even more anticipation. I had had enough of the military life—a life where others have control and my response had to be "yes, Sir." I was ready to make my own decisions and live with the results.

Freedom to be me

My personal story is unique and at the same time generational. Many of my common childhood experiences may mirror the experiences of many or most of the other 75,999,999 U.S. baby boomers. My childhood, in some sense, was their childhood. Although unable to speak for them, I have cracked opened the door to their past so that they may reflect and think about their childhood. Reflecting back on my childhood and writing about it caused some soul searching. I am an accepting person and have never wished my childhood would have been different. It was what is was and at this point my childhood experiences can only be used to help me understand how they shaped and formed me. Clearly my free-range childhood helped prepare me for the adult portion of my life.

Living in at least six different homes and being part of a large family taught me that uncertainty is okay. I did not ask for, nor was I given, specific parental direction in life. For instance, my parents exposed me to religion rather than force me into one. Life is about making choices. I was given the freedom to make my own and then live with the results. This was very liberating for me because it taught me to think for myself rather than worry about and attempt to live up to the expectations of others. I was given the freedom to be me—not the mirror image of someone else. I now believe knowing at an early age exactly what a person wants to do with his or her life will cause that person to miss some great opportunities to learn over the course of his or her lifetime. Without certainty or clear direction, my life has been a meandering and joyful learning journey. The lack of structure and freedom given to me during my childhood allowed me to explore the world around me and learn as I journeyed forward. The independence I was given, intentionally or unintentionally, made me think for myself, make decisions, and learn about and accept the broader world.

Moving around as a child, along with my time in the military, exposed me to new places and people and made me more accepting and tolerant of others. If I had grown up in one place and stayed there as an adult I would be living in a small, narrow world shackled with prejudices and beliefs that would blind me to the plight of others in the broader world. The hardships faced while growing up strengthened me. They taught me about life and allow me to display compassion when others face struggles in their own lives. Growing up both with a father who had an alcohol dependency problem and in a large family with a lack of financial resources were two positive learning experiences. They strengthened my resolve to be different, to not worry about the things out of my control, and to always remain optimistic about the future. Fate would not decide my future—I would.

In some respects, my life's journey has been a bit like playing five-card draw poker. I initially had to play the hand I was dealt. But then, like each of you, I had the opportunity to exchange a few cards for some new ones to hopefully better my position. I do believe I turned a mediocre hand into a winning hand. This was only possible because of all the special people who have been part of my purposeful life. You know who you are.

Chapter References

Family and Place

Joliet, IL. (2005). In *Encyclopedia of Chicago*. Retrieved January 5, 2017 from https://goo.gl/94sLMt

It Takes Faith to be an Angel

Home (n.d.) In *Welcome to the Joliet Santa Fortunata website*. Retrieved March 8, 2017 from jolietsantafortunata.com

A Handful of Worm Poop

Kennedy march (2017, February 18). In *Wikipedia, The Free Encyclopedia*. Retrieved May 24, 2017, from https://goo.gl/juKDvL

And Here's the Beatles

Dylan, B. (1964). *The Times They Are a-Changin'*. Retrieved May 24, 2017 from https://goo.gl/zxWyLv

Crystal radio. (2017, May 19). In *Wikipedia, The Free Encyclopedia*. Retrieved May 24, 2017, from https://goo.gl/fKkN9f

The Zombies. (1967, August). *Time of the Season*. Retrieved May 24, 2017 from https://goo.gl/cPWrZp

Going Up the Country. (2017, May 20). In *Wikipedia, The Free Encyclopedia*. Retrieved May 26, 2017, from https://goo.gl/Nptjjb

About the Author

Robert Hafey currently resides in Homer Glen, Illinois, not far from the city of Joliet which was the setting for much of *Boomhood*. Most of his work career was in the field of manufacturing until he started a successful consulting business in 2010. While traveling for business on a flight from Melbourne to Sydney, Australia, a conversation with a woman seated next to him motivated him to write this memoir. Their conversation revealed Hafey had already written a successful technical book related to his consulting work and she had completed a non-fiction manuscript and was returning from a writer's conference in Melbourne where she had been actively seeking a publisher. This back and forth conversation about writers and writing was inspiring and not forgotten for after completing a second technical book the process of writing this memoir began. For 2-1/2 years the stories of his childhood were written and re-written. He had the time of his life writing this memoir and he hopes reading it will trigger memories of your childhood.

www.ingramcontent.com/pod-product-compliance
Lightning Source LLC
Chambersburg PA
CBHW021126300426
44113CB00006B/311